stop
bitching
start
pitching

stop
bitching
start
pitching

marty kellard & ian elliot

the 9 success steps to winning business

PIER

9

{ dedications }

Personally

For Ian that's Lincoln, Cameron and Suzie, and
for Marty that's Laura.

Professionally

To the three people who passed on their knowledge to us: Peter Rogen,
who came out from New York in 1983 to teach us about presentation
skills (the 'how' to say it) and Geoff Cousins and Alex Hamill, our
predecessors, mentors, and past chairmen of that wonderful ad agency,
George Patterson Advertising, who taught us our pitching skills
(the 'what, when and where' to say it).

contents

foreword 06

introduction 08

1

rumble 24

2 mumble 46

3

bumble 59

4

stumble 100

5 stagger 130

walk 156

6

7

8

run 176

jump 184

9

fly 188

epilogue 199

appendixes 206

{ foreword }

Ian Elliot and Marty Kellard are the two best new business winners
I've ever seen. When we worked together at George Patterson's,
Australia's largest advertising agency, they won over
A$250 million in new business over a four-year period.

In a business where a 25 per cent success rate is seen as pretty
good (because there are usually four to six competitors each time),
they achieved a winning rate of 78 per cent. Often they were
virtually unbeatable, even when they started from a position that
seemed unwinnable.

The techniques they used can be applied to any business that wants to win.

These guys are good.

Alex Hamill
(past Chairman and CEO of George Patterson Advertising)

{ introduction }

before anything

'The secret of all success is constancy of purpose.'
Benjamin Disraeli

Jerry Seinfeld does a great comedy sketch on the difference between winning and losing in a 100-metre race. He just turns side-on to his audience and says that the difference between first and second is between this ... and this, as he sticks his neck forward a fraction. Back here you're a loser; out here you're a winner. Looks funny and is funny. Yet all the winner did was stick his neck out and got the prize.

It's an old truth that everyone remembers the winner and no one remembers the poor guy who came second. It's an old truth but it's not totally true—because the guy who came in second sure remembers it. So if you like, this book is about sticking your neck out and winning.

You know that winning in business isn't easy. Every buck is hard fought for these days. Every contract that comes up for pitch, every opportunity you have to land a new client, and every new tender document is a chance to put you and your company ahead of your competitors.

The trouble is that it's our experience that most businesses, whether they're banks, law firms, ad agencies, engineering contractors, printers, telcos, freight forwarders or any other kind of organisation you can think of, just don't have the systems and processes that make winning more certain and losing less likely.

Just as importantly, they don't have the attitude that's needed to win. Most businesses don't follow strict procedures or practices that guarantee them the best chance of success, and few have a winning attitude ingrained in their culture. Well, those systems, practices, attitude and culture are what this book is all about.

WHY THE TITLE?

The reason this book is called *Stop Bitching, Start Pitching* is simply this: we've observed over the years that whenever anyone loses a pitch there's always a reason, and often a string of them. 'We were beaten on price. Those guys cut the guts out of it. They'll never make money on it. We'd never stoop that low', through to 'We were never in with a chance, it turns out that their MD and Company A's MD are old school mates. They play golf every weekend'. All are terribly plausible and, to most, believable excuses. But absolute bullshit! The only reason you didn't win is because you weren't good enough.

'What!?', you say. 'No way. We were good enough. We know for a fact that our offering was superior, our price more than competitive and on the day we were on fire. We presented brilliantly. We were more than good enough.' Well, here's the rub. You're probably right on all those counts, but you weren't good enough ... at pitching. A superior product and price—well presented—play only a small part in pitching. Those ingredients are only the price of entry, and without them you don't deserve a ticket to the party.

Presenting a superior offering well is not pitching. Pitching is about understanding all of the dynamics at play in the market—your competitors, the client's business strategy and the individual needs stated and unstated, emotional and rational, human and corporate of all the decision makers and influencers—and then doing everything you need to do to win.

The working title of this book was 'Everything is winning'. A clever title we thought that plays on the 'winning is everything' phrase. It's also a much more accurate and articulate description of what this book's about. The fact is that in order to win, you have to do absolutely *everything* right. But if we used that title, you probably wouldn't be reading this book. It would be gathering dust on a shelf or in the $2 bin at the bookshop.

You see, we know that you want to win and in the past you've probably been disappointed on the occasions when you didn't. We know that you've probably bitched about it with some of the same excuses above. We know that you take winning seriously and you hate losing. It's bad for your ego and it's bad for your career. We understand the commercial, personal, rational, emotional, tactical and strategic needs you have concerning pitching and provided a hook in the title that appealed to *you* on every one of those levels. We've never met you. But we know you. You bought the book didn't you?

So, the point of this book is to get you to understand the genuine needs, stated and unstated, of the company and, more importantly, the human beings in the company who will make and influence the decision to appoint you. Then, and only then, if you have your superior product and value proposition well presented in a framework that demonstrates you understand and can positively influence *all* of those needs better than your competitors, you will win.

BUT WHY LISTEN TO US?

You might ask what qualifications do we have to talk about this, what have we done to earn the right to give you our ideas on the principles to follow in winning business? Well, we worked in advertising for thirty years. We worked together side by side for twenty of those years and were involved in hundreds of pitches. In the last five years of working together we'd refined our system down to such a degree that we won 35 out of 45 pitches. That's a success rate of 77.7 per cent.

And being the biggest agency we were pitching the biggest accounts. Wins like Hyundai, the Sydney 2000 Olympics, Bushells, Star City Hotel and Casino, Ansett Airlines and dozens of others. Usually we were up against between three and five other agencies. So on average we should have won between 17 and 25 per cent, all other things being equal.

What gave us the edge? Well, hopefully our work was superior and our value proposition was more compelling. But in a business where it's difficult to prove the superiority of your ideas before they're put into practice, the reason we won so consistently is because we understand the dynamics of the pitch process better than our competitors.

Many of our competitors thought that the way to win was to solve the client's problem. Our view was that we first needed to solve our problem, and our problem was we didn't have the account!

THE BEST IDEA RARELY WINS—THE BEST PITCH WINS

Once you've won the account then you can create meaningful solutions for that client by working in concert with them. But you can't make great ads (or anything else) for clients you haven't got.

So, step one: win the account. The greatest political leaders have always understood this fact—first task: get elected. Every business pitch is different, but every one of them has to face the same simple problem: how do you find the way to stick your neck out in front when it counts?

The Victory Virus

Winning is infectious. You know it because you've felt it. Think about the times you've been in a winning team, and how the whole thing takes on a certain inevitability. You just know you're going to win. Your opposition sees you as winners before you even get onto the field. You have the edge mentally and you get on a roll.

The same thing happens in business. Successful businesses get good at winning. They get used to it and they learn to expect it. Also, people want to play for the winning team, so it makes it easier to recruit the best players, which further weakens the opposition.

This all creates a 'winning culture', which is a whole lot better than a 'losing culture'—but which is just as easy to get into. We know a business that had a batting average of 5 per cent. They won one out of twenty accounts in two years. How do you think those guys felt going into a pitch? It's remarkable they even turned up on the day, since it seems like they were waiting for a lottery win: 'Maybe this will be the one day in twenty we win a prize ...'

But while we'll teach you everything you need to say and how to say it to give you the best chance of winning, there is one thing we can't teach you—and you either have it or you don't …

Attitude

There's an attitude that people in winning businesses have. Geoffrey Cousins, past Chairman of George Patterson Advertising, described it as 'arrogance cloaked in humility'. If your business doesn't seem to have a winning culture, then have a look at the attitude of the people at the top. Including you. You have to exude a fearlessness and a confidence that says: 'We will win, we will prevail'.

There was some fascinating proof of that at the 'What Makes a Champion' conference that was organised to coincide with the Sydney 2000 Olympics. One of our mentors, past Chairman of George Patterson's, champion businessman and triathlete, Alex Hamill, was asked to be the MC for the conference. He had to take careful note of what each speaker said, and find a way of linking that speaker to the next. (We're talking about people like Nelson Mandela, Sir Edmund Hillary, Herb Elliott and many other champions of sport, business and personal endeavour.)

The truly amazing thing that Alex discovered at the end of it all was that there was one common element that ran through every single presentation. One common theme that linked all of the speeches—no matter who gave it and no matter on what subject—and that one thing was the word 'persistence'. These champions had an attitude that said that they would prevail, whatever the odds, whatever the situation.

There's a great quote about persistence that rings as true today as it did when it was first spoken eighty years ago. It came from Calvin Coolidge, thirtieth President of the United States. He had this to say:

Nothing in the world can take the place of persistence. Talent will not; nothing is more common than unsuccessful men of talent. Genius will not; unrewarded genius is almost a proverb. Education will not; the world is full of educated derelicts. Persistence and determination alone are omnipotent.

You have to harness that power, you have to assume that cold clinical arrogance that comes from knowing you will prevail, and then you have to cloak it, just like Geoff Cousins says, in a little humility.

THE EVIDENCE IS IN THE FINGERPRINTS

You are going to discover, as you put this system of ours to work, that there are people who will be totally committed to the task, while others will hang back. This isn't just the normal definition of the 80/20 rule. This goes deeper than that.

It goes to the basic fear of failure that we all have. The old saying that goes 'Victory has a thousand fathers; defeat is an orphan' is very definitely true when it comes to winning business.

You'll find that there will be people in your business who want to be close enough to owning the problem that they will have a claim to holding the trophy if you win, but who will be just far enough removed to be able to say 'I had nothing to do with it' if you lose.

We say that you want people who are prepared to get their fingerprints all over the problem, who desperately want to be involved, and who are prepared to live or die by the results. If you fail to win and the opportunity is dead, you want to be able to dust for fingerprints. Those who were committed to winning will have their fingerprints all over the body. Similarly, when you win and hold up that trophy you want to know that everybody who had their fingerprints clearly on the task deserves to hold the Cup. Win or lose, they proudly gave it their all and were publicly committed to the battle.

You will find too that there are people who will be just as eager to go to the meetings, get involved—but not *too* involved—and end up shrugging their shoulders if you don't win: 'It wasn't my fault'. You don't want to work with people like this.

Don't worry, you will find them—they're everywhere. But happily the processes and systems we've set up will quickly reveal them, and they can be dealt with. How you deal with them is up to you.

THE FEAR FACTOR

While we're on the subject of commitment, let's talk about what your company needs from its leader on the subject of winning business.

First of all, your team needs to know that the business is hungry. All of us have received emails or memos, usually either at the start of the financial year or at the beginning of the New Year, full of blather about this being 'Our Year' and other nonsense that no one reads and nobody believes anyway. The only way to get people to truly believe you is by putting your ass on the line, making a public commitment that everyone understands.

We believe that each year true leaders should nominate a specific target for their new business wins. Don't generalise and say, 'This year we are going to win more business'. Be specific, say, 'This year we *will* win $50 million of new contracts by December'.

Now, you're probably thinking, 'Won't my staff think I (and they) have failed if we fail to achieve that?' The answer is, 'Yes'.

So why would you do such a seemingly dangerous thing? Because it does four things:

1. It clearly gives you a target to aim at. Not some amorphous feelgood 'We're gonna win', but a direct, 'We have to win $50 million'. So you can keep a scorecard and you know exactly where you stand. If, by September, you are $30 million short, well, you know what you've got to do—win that $30 mill.
2. It makes it clear to your staff that you have your fingerprints all over this thing. So they know that if you're committed then the wisest thing to do is get committed to the task themselves or get out of the way.
3. It will scare the crap out of you, so that you will be forced to win; or lose a lot of face.
4. We firmly believe that you get what you foresee. Visualise victory and you'll get it. Focus on failure and you'll get it. Playing to win is a whole different approach to playing not to lose.

Jim Collins and Jerry Porras, in their book *Built to Last* (New York: HarperBusiness, 1994), calls this kind of thinking a BHAG: a Big Hairy Audacious Goal. If you have the guts to go out there and announce that your goal is to win $50 million in new contracts, you've given yourself one hell of a BHAG.

But the wonderful thing is that it galvanises the whole business. Suddenly everyone gets it. They understand the reason why they are working back late. Giving up weekends, making sacrifices for the common good.

Adversity and extremis bring out the best in almost everyone. Winston Churchill said at the height of the London Blitz, 'They do not know it yet, but this will be the time of their lives'. It brings people together for a common goal, and can transform a company. But it takes someone to have the courage to get up and say it, and mean it.

SEND OUT A SEARCH PARTY

This may fall into the pile marked 'The Bleeding Obvious' but we will say it all the same: your company needs to have someone who has a Key Performance Indicators (KPI) labelled something like 'Win $50 million in new business'. That person could be anyone from the CEO to a specialist new business development manager. And they have to have the authority to press the button that starts your business-winning machine.

We say this because the vital task of actually looking out for business-winning opportunities is often left to everyone to do. We hear a lot of CEOs say that gaining new clients is *everyone's* job. Well, yes and no.

Yes, the whole business should be ready and primed for winning (and we'll show you how). But no, just one person has to be given the task of leading the search party. If it's everyone's job, then no one will really do it. You need someone whose KPI is transparent and measurable on new business.

And they have to have the support of everyone in the organisation to drive that business at full throttle to achieve the goal. Michael Schumacher wasn't the head of the organisation, but he had the authority and support he needed to drive the wheels off his Formula One car to win. And if he crashed? 'If you're not crashing occasionally then you're not driving fast enough.'

how it works

'Want to don't pick no cotton.'
Old slave saying from the Deep South of America

A lot of companies make a lot of noise about winning business—plenty of memos, off-site conferences and good work on a whiteboard. Everyone goes away with the feeling that 'winning business' is a very good idea and we should do it as often as we can.

Generally there are responsibilities given out and targets to be reached and everyone is happy that something is being done. There are signs of industry everywhere. Maybe something is done. People might have more meetings to work out who the 'target list' might be. Someone gets out the *Yellow Pages* and goes through all the likely industries, starting at AAA Aardvark Pty Ltd, and they draw up a list of possibilities.

People even make phone calls, hoping for a blind date with a new piece of business. Reports are sent off detailing the work done, and the outcome. Over time it becomes apparent that things don't look so good. 'This is a lot harder than we thought, people might see us but they don't want to buy.' Enthusiasm wanes and people get distracted by the urgent day to day. Prospecting and presenting slowly become less of a priority. Or perhaps there's a live lead—a real pitch with a real prospect. Someone is asked to 'put the pitch together' and they do their best to bring together the right team, say all the right things and have a neat presentation. They pitch, they do their best and then they pray.

They don't win, they come 'a very close second'. But there's always another chance, right? But this failure breeds dissent, discussion, muttering in the corridor. The people aren't happy. 'We should really do better at winning business', someone senior says. And, about eighteen months after the last off-site, another conference is called and it starts all over again.

Well, this book aims to stop that cycle of pointless presentations and gloomy grumblings. Stop bitching and start pitching the right way— with a system, a purpose, a focus and a clear understanding of what it takes to have the best chance of winning.

This book isn't about prospecting for business—although the methods used here can help you in that as well. Prospecting is a skill for another discussion. This book is about what to do when you get the chance to be in a pitch and you want the best plan to ensure that you win.

It's not simply about pitching either. A lot of emphasis has been placed on Pitch Doctors over the past decade and there are some great ones out there. There are parts of this book on pitch doctoring, but it's just a small part of what this book is about.

Once you've decided *what* to say in your pitch, a good Pitch Doctor will coach you to deliver that message brilliantly, but *how* to say is only a part of what we do. We also look at *who* says it, *when* and *where*.

THE NINE STEPS

This is the step-by-step guide. In just nine steps you get from the very first meeting to the final presentation. Nine steps that guarantee you will miss no opportunity, hit every target and maximise your chance of winning. Each of these nine steps is expanded upon and set out in detail, chapter by chapter, as you get closer to the pitch.

1

step one: rumble

You rumble through the brief, select the team and begin
planning the process

2

step two: mumble

You mumble out some possible answers

3

step three: bumble

You bumble through some interviews,
then review your possible answers
against this new information

4

step four: stumble

You stumble through a rough agenda and work out your hook

5

step five: stagger

You do a rough stagger through the theatre,
your props and presentation tools

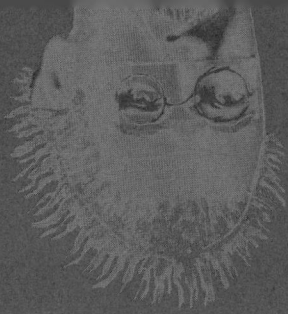

step six: walk

You do a long steady walk through the pitch with the pitch doctor reviewing your presentation

step seven: run

You do a run through, like a dress rehearsal, before a panel of judges with interests and prejudices similar to the real jury you will face

step eight: jump

Now you jump in and change, move and refine your presentation based on the jury's verdict

step nine: fly

Now you have a final fly through immediately before the pitch

then you pitch...

The following timeline sets out the meeting pointers for the stages that will get you to presentation day. Even if all you ever did with this book was use these pointers, you'd still be a mile in front of any other competing business. And if you follow the nine steps then you have a very good chance of being on the winning side.

The goals you need to achieve in each of the nine steps are as follows:

1. rumble ▶▶

Swot Team gathers information

- Top Guns meet to select team
- Decide who is Pitch Leader, Pitch Manager, Pitch Doctor and Scribe
- Swot Team is engaged
- Create a timeline

2. mumble ▶▶

Flag-fall possible answer

- 'James Bond' debrief
- Team hears from Swot Team
- Top Guns take a stab at the answer
- Decide whether to proceed
- Determine what alliances we have
- Decide budget

3. bumble ▶▶

Interviews completed, answer reviewed

- Our internal jury considered
- Determine who interviews who
- What have we learnt from the interviews?
- Nicknames for their judging panel given
- Clarify the brief and real problem
- Remember that 'every child wins a prize' and determine prize
- 'Why will they, why won't they?'
- What could we possibly say or do to win?
- Does our answer sound right?
- Decide what's pitched before and after the pitch

4. stumble ▶▶

Agenda worked out and hook created

- Create the agenda
- Work out what, how, when and who
- Timings are given
- Everyone talks through their presentation
- What's missing?
- How is the flow?
- Pitch Doctor gives feedback
- Pitch Leader decides what to add or subtract
- The hook is decided based on the best answer

5. stagger ▶▶

Timings in place, Q & A

- Work out the venue
- Decide what props to use
- All props and equipment are used and checked

6. walk ▶▶

The cockpit check

- All presentations are now written and walked through
- Pitch Doctor comments
- Pitch Leader decides
- Is there a 'push in the back'?
- Factor in any intelligence gained about competition
- Determine any 'dirty tricks'
- Cross-check brief with your agenda

7. run ▶▶

First dress rehearsal

- Assemble all players including judges
- All intros and outros worked out
- Jury watches and deliberates
- Tough Q & A
- Debrief Pitch Leader
- Get verdict

8. jump ▶▶

Jury reviews

- What needs changing?
- Last chance for 'push in the back'
- Postitive feedback
- Take photos as mementos

9. fly

The big day

- In the pitch room one hour prior to the pitch fly through everything in the third person
- Decide to win!

then you pitch...

{ meetings }

The timeline meetings have got to have outcomes—therefore, the participants have got to have a clear understanding that whatever is decided will be facilitated. They need to know the business will fast-track whatever needs to be done to enable the players to do or get whatever is required.

Every meeting has to have the right people in it. How often have you thought to yourself, 'I don't need to be in this meeting'? A lot of times, we bet. So it's vital that great care is given at the start of the process to put the right time in the right diaries. If a key player is asked to a meeting, they've got to know they have a vital role to play. Because you can bet that if you waste their time, then next time a timeline meeting is in their diary they won't be quite so interested in turning up.

2

7

4

3

6

9

5

8

1 **rumble**

{ step 1. rumble }

people buy people

'When you cast the actors, you've done much of
the work ... the casting process is crucial.'
Robert Wise

In a pitch there's one simple truth: They are buying and you are selling.
('They' being the company you're pitching to.) Whether they buy from you
will depend on Who, What, When, Where and How you say it. So the first
question in the first meeting you have is 'Who says it?'

CASTING THE PARTS

Casablanca is one of the greatest movies of all time. Great script, great
music and Bogart doing what Bogart does best, which is play Bogart.
Would it be the same movie if Ronald Reagan had played the part?
According to a Warner Bros press release, he was seriously considered,
they had him under contract and he wanted to do it but couldn't make
himself available at the time.

So They Settled on Bogie

And an interesting note (which will become relevant when later we
talk about the theatre of your pitch), you should also know that they had no
idea how to finish the movie and the last line by Claude Rains, 'This could
be the start of a beautiful friendship ...', was made up on the spot.

But why does all this matter to you? Because perhaps the key
decision that you will take is this one: Who's on our team? Who do we cast?

You might think that solving the problem would be the biggie, and of
course it's important that you have a great answer, but most of the time

people buy people. If Company A (that's who we'll call the company you're pitching to right through this book) has faith that your people can work with them, then even if your answer isn't spot on, you'll still get the win. Because the chemistry was right—and it's chemistry that casting is all about.

Learn from Hollywood

Over the last fifteen years the biggest star in Hollywood has been Tom Cruise. He hasn't won any Oscars, but his films have made a lot of money, which in the end is all that really counts to the people who really count in Hollywood. They don't count awards, they count dollars. And yes they definitely want to win the Academy Award for Best Picture, but that's because it'll make the film more money, add prestige to their company ... and make them more money.

Is Tom Cruise the Best Actor? You might have your opinion, we might have ours (we think the award goes to Sean Penn), but if we wanted to make sure the public bought our film, we'd go with Tom every time. If only casting was that easy.

Well, actually it *is* that easy. Because all you need to do is know *who* your audience (Company A) will buy from. In Hollywood, when good guys such as Tom Hanks (*Road to Perdition*) or Denzel Washington (*Training Day*) play bad guys the studios let them do it with fingers crossed. Sometimes it comes off—the movie makes money (like Tom in *Road*); but more often it doesn't (Denzel in *Day*). And yes, he won the Oscar but the film still stank—of stale popcorn because no one bought that either. Like it or not, the audience want to see their favourite stars being good guys. It all comes down to what the audience wants to see and hear, and the same thing applies to your audience, which is why you need to ask yourself this question ...

WHO FITS THE PART?

A lot of businesses believe that the same four of five people are the right people to look after the task of winning the big contract. A lot of businesses are dead wrong.

Every audience is different, because every company is different.

So the question is, 'Who will they buy from?' That doesn't just come down to which of your team have the right competencies or titles—it's about what they look like, how they talk, how they empathise with the audience, their confidence levels and a bunch of other things that will either win over your audience or have them squirming in their seats.

Who's in the Audience?

When you sit in a presentation as part of the audience, what do you think about? If it's a good presentation you're conscious of a feeling of empowerment and enjoyment. You think, 'These people are good'. You might also think a bunch of other things too—mostly to do with the flow, the ideas, and the spirit of the team doing the presentation. But it all comes back to those people.

You respect them. You listen with empathy because they are empathetic in turn. They somehow have connected with you and you are willing to buy what they are selling. In short, you believe them. Now reverse that thinking when you consider the audience you will be talking to.

- Who will give them that feeling that you have felt in the past?
- Who will make them feel comfortable?
- Who will they believe?
- Finally, who will they buy from?

The simple answer is that you have to know the people in your audience, and the company they work for. At this stage you don't know them well, you might only know them by reputation, but you should know them well enough to be able to answer these questions.

- Are they results-focused?
- Are they blokey?
- Is it possible they have prejudices about your business or the industry you are in?
- Is their company in a youthful business or in an established industry?

- Are there certain conventions that you suspect your audience will hold true?
- Do they reflect a cultural diversity?

The answers to those questions will help solve the problem of who to cast. Because if the CEO of Company A is a woman, there's a very good chance she will give greater consideration to a company that openly respects women for who they are and not what they are. If the financial officer in the audience is a buttoned-down guy with a very blinkered view of numbers—will he buy from your team if the person who's talking numbers takes a cavalier approach? If Company A is in a business that's full of ideas, then creative members of your team need to reflect that. Similarly, if they have experienced old hands, or smart young people, maybe you should think about reflecting that in the make-up of your team or even juxtaposing that to fill their gaps.

So you can begin to build your cast. There's going to be someone who talks the numbers; someone who'll be their leading man; someone who will look after research and so on. You need to bring these people in.

The Leading Roles

Now that the cast has been assembled, and now that you have an idea of the kind of people you're talking to, it's time to assign some vital roles. These roles aren't all members of the cast, they won't all be in your pitch, but they are the equivalent of the director, the production manager and, ultimately, the film critic.

THE PITCH LEADER

As the title implies, the Pitch Leader will be responsible for all the decisions required to win this pitch. This is the equivalent of the film director—but with a major part in the production as well.

That means that every single decision will be theirs—*every single decision*. They can of course seek advice and counsel from whoever they like, but the decision is theirs and theirs alone. What's in, what's out? Who's in, who's out? It's a tough gig, but it's also the most fun, because with everything that takes place, the Pitch Leader is in the thick of it.

So the first requirement is that they really want to do it. They will need to be honest, objective, part disciplinarian, part psychologist. They need to be happy to embrace the responsibility and theirs will be the cleanest set of fingerprints on the win or the loss—their grip is the tightest.

We explore the requirements of leadership much more fully in appendix 2 (see pages 209–21) because it is such a vital function in winning business, but know this—you can't do it if you don't really want to do it.

There's a rule of thumb that the army uses which says that about one person in twenty has within them the makings of a leader. So you need to recognise who has it in them to lead. The Big Guns who decide the cast should also have the courage to decide who is Pitch Leader, and nine times out of ten it will actually be one of them.

But now and then a Pitch Leader can come from elsewhere within the ranks. Maybe you are prepared to bet that a young star will rise to the pressure. Whoever the Pitch Leader is, the first rule, and the only one you need to remember is this—whatever this person decides is right, and we're backing them 100 per cent. There can be no whispering in corridors, no second-guessing and no regrets afterwards.

The Pitch Leader needs to have the complete support of the business and be in total command of their team. The team can argue with the Pitch Leader, state their case, plead and suggest whatever they like. But if they're told no, then that's it—and nothing else matters.

If you can't guarantee that the person you choose will be able to handle that kind of responsibility, don't even think about giving them the role—because it will damage them. They will vacillate and attempt to appease all. Their people will snipe and bicker and slowly turn your winning presentation into a political nightmare.

The Pitch Leader needs to be in total command, and have the courage to believe that they are absolutely right. They need to be the one who makes the big decision: 'This is the solution we're going in with'.

They review all avenues and then push the button on the one solution that they think will win the business. Once that decision is made there is no argument; no second-guessing. That's it. Right or wrong, it's their decision. The leader also decides:

- Who will be in the presentation
- What to say in the presentation
- What will be presented
- The agenda
- The venue
- The theatre
- The hook
- The presentation itself
- Who does the follow-up

And they will live or die by the result—and everybody in the business knows it. They will also have the courage to give someone—anyone who needs it—the 'push in the back', which is:

How Not to Win a Gold Medal

You may or may not remember Mary Decker Slaney. She was one of the great athletes of her generation. She held seven American records in running in distances from 800 metres to 10,000 metres. At the 1983 Helsinki World Championships she won both the 1500 and the 3000 metres. She should have won a number of Olympic gold medals and been remembered for standing on the victor's podium. Instead she's famous for falling over.

Back in 1984 she was the biggest name in athletics coming into the 1984 Los Angeles Olympics. If anyone was a certainty for a gold medal it was her in the 3000 metres. The Soviet Bloc hadn't turned up, so their steroid-fuelled frauleins from East Germany weren't going to steal any gold away from the clean Americans. Mary D was the nearest thing you could get to a lay-down certainty. Except that she was the one who was laid down.

By Zola Budd. Remember her? Waif-like runner from South Africa who was famous for running without shoes. She was good too, but no one seriously thought she'd be a problem for Mary. Mary certainly didn't think so anyway.

But come the day of the race, with Mary Decker running strongly near the front of the pack with 800 metres to go, Zola Budd makes a lightning run around the outside of the field, gets just in front of Mary and then slows down slightly.

It puts Mary off her stride, she clips Zola Budd's heels, trips and falls and now the memory that's forever etched in our minds is of that tortured face crying in fury, anguish and pain as she writhes on the track—her dream gone forever.

Right after those LA Olympics in 1984 there was a worldwide management conference of our company in New York City. Geoff Cousins, our company Chairman at the time, found a Mary Decker lookalike to use in his presentation on new business skills. He interviewed her on stage and when he asked 'Mary Decker' what she would have done differently she said simply this: 'I'd push that bitch right in the back'.

Let Budd fall over, let Mary win, just get out of the way.

The Pitch Leader has to know when to give someone the 'push in the back'. The people who are involved in the pitch have to understand that the push in the back isn't personal—it's simply that you can't afford to be polite, to let someone continue to believe they are a part of the presentation. Don't be afraid to say 'Sorry, but we've cut your part'.

Push them in the back and give yourself the chance to win. It takes courage, it takes humanity to do it well, but if everyone understands that the Pitch Leader needs to make the tough calls then it will be done.

The hardest push in the back is the one where the person involved has done a lot of the work, and there's a tendency to want them to get the reward of a role on the big day. We've been pushed in the back by the Pitch Leader, even when we held the lofty titles of National Creative Director, Chief Executive and Chairman. Why?

Because it was right for the pitch. The Pitch Leader was able to make the call and tell us why we weren't right to play this particular part in this particular performance. And we accepted it. And in each instance he was right and we won.

Sadly, there's nothing right or fair about winning. You just have to know what is right for the success of the group, and no matter how hard some poor bastard has worked—if they're not right for the part, push them in the back. That way you'll have a clear run at the gold. (Mary Decker never won an Olympic medal of any colour.)

We still hear of presentations where the room is stacked with those whose efforts or titles got them a seat at the table even when they didn't have a genuine role. Our rule is that the only reason you're in the room is because if you aren't, we might lose.

So that's the Pitch Leader—a big job, but the most exciting role you can play in business.

THE PITCH MANAGER

The one person responsible for making everything happen is the Pitch Manager, a role similar to the production manager on a film set. They need to be very task-orientated, because they will be responsible for the entire presentation. Think of them as the officer responsible for all the tools, materials, resources and timings required to make the pitch happen.

They are responsible for organising all the meetings and making certain that every diary is coordinated. They are responsible for all the budgetary requirements. They hold the purse strings, but very importantly they don't decide how it's spent or what it is spent on—that's the job of the Pitch Leader.

No, all we want from the Pitch Manager is perfection—everything has to happen on time, on budget, with the right people doing the right things right on time. No surprises!

You have to think that this means the Pitch Manager of your dreams is going to be one heck of a worker—probably doesn't mind putting people's noses out of joint, because they have the authority to get things done. And of course that clearly depends on your whole business understanding that the Pitch Manager *does* have the authority, and everyone understands the role of Pitch Manager.

THE PITCH DOCTOR

The Pitch Doctor is the second most important player in the whole presentation. They play a role that's similar to a great film critic. They're the person who looks at the presentation in its entirety and decides whether it's working or not.

So what Should the Pitch Doctor be Good at?

Well, first they need to be able to see things from the mindset of the customer. They have to be sure that the whole performance flows. They need to be confident that every point is presented in a logical way, with the most potent delivery possible. And they need to be able to do it to every seat in the room. Which means they need to be able to understand what the important issues are—for every member of the audience. This is where it's imperative that you have a clear picture of each member of the judging panel—and we'll be covering that in chapter 3 'Bumble'.

The Pitch Doctor needs to have the ability to read each part of the presentation from the point of view of every member of the audience: 'If that is said in that manner, how will it impact on each individual member of the audience?' (Not just the person who it's aimed at.) Therefore, the Pitch Doctor needs to have a great deal of empathy, because it is a very creative task to be able to assume the mindset of a variety of people—and to do so in a way that still allows for clear-headed judgments to take place.

The same degree of empathy and understanding is required in the way the Pitch Doctor looks at each individual who has a role in the presentation—and here it's important for the Pitch Doctor to themselves be a very good presenter. (This is because they need to understand what works and what doesn't work, and the best way of saying it.) And if, in their opinion, the message isn't being delivered effectively, or correctly, then they need to be able to explain what exactly needs to be done to change that part of the presentation. This needs to be done in consultation with the Pitch Leader—who will always make the final decision.

The Pitch Doctor needs to be proactive and capable of giving honest feedback, but with compassion and understanding. They're trying to gain the best performance from the cast—so diplomacy and the ability to read people are vital.

They'll also need to be eagle-eyed for all the little mistakes that can creep into a presentation and remain undiscovered until it's too late. These can be as simple as a spelling mistake to a logo that is out of date, or a person's title that has changed on the client side.

We've found that the Pitch Doctor is better used if they are close to the problem, but not too close. In other words they understand very clearly what the problem is and what needs to be solved (at every level) but aren't too involved in the actual solution itself. This helps give objectivity, and you need that objectivity to be crystal clear in your decision-making.

But there's one more thing that needs to be confirmed once again— the Pitch Doctor can recommend anything, but it's the Pitch Leader who decides. It always ends with the Pitch Leader!

THE SCRIBE

We strongly believe that every meeting must have a Scribe. The Scribe will have a continuing role throughout this process, not just in the meetings prescribed in the nine steps timeline (see pages 20–2) , but also in interviews with the clients, right through to the presentation itself. So let's quickly explain the role of the Scribe.

The Scribe's job, at least in the timeline meetings, is to make certain that there is an accurate record of all that is said, all who said it, objections, discussions, questions and so on. (You want to be able to have a summary of everything that was covered.) While you might think that you'll be taking notes and presumably everyone else in the meeting will be doing the same, you're still going to be missing the big picture. The Scribe's role is to make certain that everything is covered—not just individual actions, but everything.

The Scribe can be an enthusiastic PA, or anyone else who has a keen ear and a degree of perseverance, because it isn't an easy task. It's easy to get distracted. The Scribe has to be able to focus and to listen accurately. But the key thing is that the Scribe doesn't participate. They know that their role is very clear—to have a precise record of who said what, what was discussed, what was decided and what questions needed answering. Once the Scribe has transcribed the notes, these can be issued as bullet points to the team members so that everyone knows what was said, what was promised and who promised it.

Bring in the Swot Team

We've all heard of great business opportunities being won by the unlikeliest of competitors. How did they win that? Well, very often the reason is pretty straightforward—old mates repaying debts, the level of security or insecurity the CEO feels, sometimes it's even an attractive payoff, such as promising a round of golf with Greg Norman or Tiger Woods.

None of that has anything to do with how good your competitor's answer was. But it has a lot to do with how well they knew who they were pitching to and what would really sway the decision. Your aim is to never be beaten like that again, because we'll give you the ammunition to counteract that kind of stuff.

You need knowledge. Using a Swot Team is how you do it. There should be at least two people who make up the Swot Team and they should have a capacity for intelligent, disciplined work under pressure. They should also have a clear idea of what they're looking for and they should be able to deliver it in a cogent, informative manner. What you don't want are people who get distracted, or who want to add their own interpretation of what they're discovering. That isn't their job.

So what is the job of the Swot Team? Well, they're going to swot up on everything they can find out about the client and the problem and the people in question. Let us assume that the brief has come in so that in fifteen days time you have to present your answer to why your business should have Company A's contract. You need to find out everything there is to know about Company A. Not just what they have written in the brief, but everything about them—the structure of their business, their competitors and competitive activity, their share price fluctuations, industry trends, who are their key executives and board members, plus everything else you need to know to solve their problem, stated and unstated.

Just as importantly, you need to know whatever you can about the people who will be in the room on presentation day. You need to know whether there is harmony in the ranks, or whether there's a power play going on. Does the CEO feel safe, or are they under threat? Does their Finance person have a good relationship with the CEO? What industry and competitive threats is the company facing?

Many of these questions will need further exploration as we go further into the nine steps, but the very first thing the Swot Team needs to do is create a database that has as much information as possible to enable your business to come up with the solution to Company A's problem. That can include information gathered through publicly available desk research, to inside knowledge gathered from contacts, to specific research you've conducted yourselves.

Where do they find the information? Most of it will be in the public record. Look for press releases and annual reports, websites, analyst presentations, copies of senior executives' speeches and company brochures. Visit their customers. Gather, gather, gather.

If important members of their company have been interviewed in the business press, or have published articles, what did those articles say? The internet is a great source to look for speeches made by the key people—what did those speeches say? What concerns them that they've made public? What language/terms do they use repeatedly? Because your solutions need to echo that language and address those terms. If the CEO has been seen on TV, what did they look like, what did they sound like, how did they act and what did they say? Maybe just as importantly, what didn't they say?

The Swot Team creates a dossier on the company—its strengths, weaknesses, opportunities and threats, as well as a snapshot of the Key Players who will either be in the presentation or will influence the final decision.

This whole period of work should take from two to five days. At the end of that period the Swot Team does the 'James Bond Debrief ' (see chapter 2 'Mumble') and distributes their findings in bullet points to all the key players. The amount of this pre-reading should be as concise as possible, but the detailed evidence needs to be available for deeper analysis.

the road to winning

'The secret of all victory lies in the organisation of the non-obvious.'
Marcus Aurelius

As you can see in this first meeting—the 'Rumble' on our timeline— a bunch of things have to be decided. The last thing that must be mapped out is the rest of our timeline, because things need to happen in a natural sequence to a disciplined timeframe.

So first, let's explain why you need a timeline in the first place; what it should be; what you should expect from it and what outcomes it should deliver.

'I HAVEN'T GOT TIME TO DO A TIMELINE'

Our timeline is simply a schedule that results from a 'call to action' (the brief) that allows specific tasks to be performed in a specific way to achieve your ultimate goal. It has an agreed-upon minimum, optimum and maximum duration for each of the procedures that need to be followed to ensure success, and is tracked through meetings.

It also needs to be set in stone. Therefore, everyone has to understand how important it is. The top brass can't get out of a meeting when it is set up, because as soon as those people are seen to treat the timeline as a 'like to' rather than a 'need to', you'll quickly find everyone else down the line having equally good reasons why they can't make that meeting either.

The timeline is set out the way it is so that you can get your best resources available when you need them: for research; for solving the problem; for rehearsals; and much else besides. So here are some suggestions for getting the most out of your timeline and the participants in each of its segments.

Decisions

Decisions need to be made quickly. Therefore make sure that each meeting has a rigid timeframe with a rigid structure and stick to it. Because you know that you can't spin the wheels for too long, it forces action to be taken. You know you have to make this decision in this meeting. It forces you to think and to deliver impetus to the troops.

Positive Results

Because there is a flow to the timeline, people can see they are making progress—they have a yardstick to measure their contribution.

They also know that in this team environment, if one person isn't pulling their weight, the others are asked to carry a heavier load. The non-contributors are exposed. But countering that is the fact that every participant can see the effect their role has on the whole, and the result is a positive feeling of teamwork—of the whole being greater than the sum of its parts. They can feel the gathering momentum and they can catch the scent of victory.

Follow Meeting Rules

How many meetings have you been in where you felt like no one was in control, no one knew why they were there, and no decision was made? In fact, how many meetings have you been to that could be summarised by, 'Well, that was a complete waste of time'?

Our timeline can help eliminate that problem, because first and foremost you know the exact reason for the meeting, and you know the precise outcome you're aiming for. Our suggestion is that every meeting has a leader, the Pitch Leader in fact, who sets out exactly the time limits of the meeting and the outcomes desired. Every meeting ends with a clear agreement on what was decided and every meeting ends with a clear distribution of responsibilities. (See appendix 1, pages 206–9, for more information on the dos and don'ts of meetings.)

If you want a great example of why timelines work, here's one that worked big time.

WHY D-DAY WASN'T E-DAY

As you probably know, the original date in 1944 for D-Day, the Invasion of Europe in World War II, was actually 5 June, not 6 June. But weather was too adverse to launch the attack.

The weather forecasts for the 6th weren't much better, but the combination of tides and the moon made it vital that either they go right then or wait another few weeks, with all the dangers which that delay could have brought into play.

Supreme Allied Commander Dwight D. Eisenhower made the call, at 4.15 am on 5 June, 'OK, we'll go', and the rest is, well, history.

But when he made that decision, he did so in the knowledge that everything in the lead-up to that day that could have been done to ensure success had been done. The right commanders were in place who had all been given the right information, based on the best intelligence they could gather. They had the right equipment and they had clear and concise objectives. The further up the ranks you went, the more you knew the details of the invasion and its ultimate aim. The further down the ranks you went, the less you knew of the details, but the more you knew of your own specific task.

The point of all this is that the Allies were following a detailed timeline. They knew they couldn't get to their ultimate aim without making sure meticulous process was followed along the way.

The same thinking applies in winning the victory you're after in your business. The difference is that nobody dies. Their lives were at risk; all we can lose is our lifestyle. So just as the Allies had a goal in mind, and a date in time that led to that goal, so too *you* have a goal in mind, and you need to have a timeline to get you there.

This is all about military precision; about accumulating intelligence; about trusting your troops and infusing them with the power of a great purpose and a great vision—but it all starts, rather prosaically, with a simple timeline.

What Happens First?

We can assume you have a date in the diary when you are being asked to make your presentation, or to tender your document. This date is usually dictated by the prospect, although that isn't always the case.

The timeline we've included at the front of the book (see pages 20–2) works to a three-week schedule and is set out with our nine steps. Obviously, if you have more time you can expand certain areas, and equally if it's a shortened timeframe then you have to collapse these suggested timings.

The only requirement that's absolutely locked in stone is that you have a timeline and that everybody who you want involved in this victory knows it.

So, after you've chosen your team and defined who does what, the very next thing you do, knowing your deadline, is work out your timeline, using our template to do so. Each one of those nine points should be on it, with the last point obviously being the day of the pitch.

But maybe you're thinking: 'Why do I need a timeline? I know what needs to be done and I know who can do it. We can do this without such pressures'. Now it's possible that you aren't thinking this. However, from our experience there must be an awful lot of people who do think that way, because we've seen an awful lot of badly planned, ill-judged presentations, where rehearsals are done in the cab. And for the most part, they don't win.

Talking in Code

We've talked about D-Day. It's a good example (we hope) of the role of the timeline. But it's also not a bad example of another element to this whole process, and that's the language that you and your team will use.

We don't mean swearing at each other (not recommended but occasionally inevitable), we mean that everyone should understand the 'language' and the 'code words' of the process, as well as all the other elements involved in carrying off the ultimate prize.

We all know how vital code words were in World War II. In fact D-Day itself is a great example of the use of code words and the great lengths that were taken to ensure their secrecy—and their meaning.

For instance, on 2 May 1944, the London *Daily Telegraph* crossword puzzle had this question: 'One of the US', with the answer being 'Utah'. On 12 May an answer was 'Omaha' and on different days up until the beginning of June 'Overlord', 'Mulberry' and 'Neptune' were all answers to these *Daily Telegraph* crossword puzzles. Since all of these words were secret code words for various aspects of the D-Day operation, MI5 got involved and eventually sent two agents to have a quiet word with the man who wrote the puzzles. His name was Sidney Dawes, a schoolteacher—and the part that worried the agents was that his brother-in-law was a highly placed Admiralty official.

Dawes had no simple explanation. It must all have been a coincidence. And so after checking the facts the whole thing was left as one of those strange coincidences that happen in war.

It was only years later that the probable solution to why those words appeared came to light. Apparently Dawes used to set his students exercises in filling in crossword grids to help them with spelling. One of his students, a Ron French, had overheard some of the suspect words being spoken by US Army officers, and had simply used them in his crosswords.

His teacher liked the words and used them himself. After MI5 had left the school, the teachers had gone through these crosswords and found the suspect words. French was called in to the headmaster's office and was sworn to secrecy—a secret he kept until Sidney Dawes' death in 1985.

The point of this is that the words themselves weren't important—it was their *meaning*. So too in our process. There are words that will need to be understood by all your troops as well. Words and phrases like 'Scribe' and 'Swot Team' and 'push in the back'.

It's vital that your business knows this language and understands the meaning of these code words or phrases. It's a lot easier to have clear communication when everyone understands what you're talking about, which is why we suggest you make sure the language you use is clearly understood right through the business so that everybody who is touched by the new business drive understands what you mean. Then make sure you tell each person exactly what each expression means to them in the job they're doing, and the expectations that that expression conveys.

Oh, the final word on D-Day in case you ever wondered, the 'D' stood for absolutely nothing.

{ questions? }

Have you noticed how the best interviewers—
people like Michael Parkinson or Barbara
Walters—don't have a long list of questions
which they refer to? Rather they have broad
themes they want to explore (if their subject will
let them) and, most importantly, they ask
questions based on what was previously said,
which lead on from the last point or a point
made earlier. Opposite to that is the kind of
brusque interrogation where the interviewee is
subjected to a barrage of questions that are
rattled off, answered without really being
listened to, and the really interesting avenues are
ignored in pursuit of every question being asked.

PLANNING AHEAD

The very next thing that has to happen, after you've created a timeline and addressed the nine steps, is to make certain that all the right people are in place for all the right meetings—the key people in the key meetings to make the key decisions. They have to have their diaries booked in, and set like stone. No excuses.

Knowing that the business of your clients must continue, sometimes the most effective way of getting everyone on the same page of the diary is to make sure you set strict time limits. Arrange for the meetings to take place before 8 am or after 6 pm. Lunch meetings also work, and there's always the weekend.

You will notice that in step eight of our nine steps, 'Jump' (see chapter 8), the judges are people within your own business who will play the part of specific people on the client's judging panel. Over the course of the next few days you will be discovering more and more about what the client's judges are looking for in your presentation. They will have specific personal needs when they judge your solution. At this stage, you can't cast those roles, but you will need to start thinking about the people you will cast in these roles.

It's also highly desirable to have a 'War Room' that is set aside and used exclusively for all meetings leading up to winning this pitch. This room is going to be the nerve centre for the whole operation, and it should be outfitted with everything that will be required during the course of the process. It should include things like TV and video equipment, PowerPoint equipment, a whiteboard with whiteboard markers—anything and everything that you and your team will need, all in one place. All the intelligence that you've gathered lives here. Obviously security is essential and it should have a strong lock and access must be limited to those people who have an essential role to play.

On the matter of security, it is one area that is often overlooked. Make sure it is someone's responsibility to wipe off the whiteboard after every meeting. It's astonishing how often we've gone into client companies and used their whiteboard only to discover that once you hit the forward button and the next bright new sheet of whiteboard comes into view, so also comes the next quarter's business plans, or profit projections. This is all about being as professional and as focused as you would be if lives were at risk. Fortunately, lives aren't at risk, but let's face it, livelihoods are.

breathe

{ step 2. mumble }

the James Bond debrief

'There are no facts, just interpretations.'
Friedrich Nietzsche

You've seen it a hundred times, whether it's in *Mission Impossible* re-runs on TV or when M does the debrief in a James Bond movie—in a snapshot that takes about two minutes of screen time our hero is brought up to speed about the problem, the timing, the dangers and the people involved. 'Here's Dr Fat Finger', as M presses the slide button and a picture of a swarthy guy with one fat finger hailing a taxi appears on the screen. 'He's an expert in diamond smuggling using his patients' breast implants to smuggle ... etc ... etc ... etc.' You get the picture. Indeed, you've seen the picture.

Well, that's what you want now from the Swot Team—a concise picture of all the issues that have been discovered by them over the past two to five days. Use a PowerPoint presentation. Run it exactly like you've seen in those James Bond movies. The people in the room, the problem solvers, the Big Guns, are going to need a clear picture of the issues and the people they are dealing with. If the Pitch Leader is a new business development director or sales director, then the CEO and everyone else who has a capacity for positive input needs to be in this briefing, while the Scribe takes notes. The Big Guns won't necessarily play a part in the pitch itself, but they can help come up with the answer.

Use snapshots from the annual report so that everyone is very clear about who the key executives and board members are—what they look like, their history, role, interests and so on down the line. 'Here's a chart of the share price over the last five years. Notice the spike when the CEO was appointed? Look at the price now. What do we learn from that?' 'What does the brief say, exactly? What does it leave out?' The Swot Team should have everything that's ever likely to be requested on hand and ready to go. If this Company A is an advertiser, then they should have examples of their advertising, as well as copies of the advertising from their competitors. The aim is to cover everything and miss nothing.

The maximum time the James Bond debrief should last is one hour. The idea of this meeting is to make sure that the Big Guns understand the stated problem contained in the brief. But hang on a minute ...

A VITAL POINT

The brief may be the problem you've been asked to answer, but it may not be the *real problem*. The brief can often be just a smokescreen to allow Company A to see what's out there in the marketplace. (Let's face it, no matter how rigorous the security, what company really wants their problems out there for all to see?) Very often the real problem is never stated in the brief, but it's still there. The trick is to work out what it might be, and you'll be doing that in the next few days of scrutiny and interviewing.

The real problem can be something as simple as the CEO being a new appointment so they've put a rocket up everyone about revisiting all the contracts and partnerships. The real problem might be that the share price has fallen, or that a competitor has come out with a new offering.

Whatever it is, you have to understand that the brief you're working to is probably not the full problem—just part of it. The trick is to answer the brief you've been given, and at the same time, solve that real problem. Too many businesses settle for solving the stated problem and lose to someone who could see the big picture and solved the real problem.

BIG GUNS, BIG PICTURE, BIG PLANS

So what do you expect from the Big Guns, now that the Swot Team has given them the issues, the people and the opportunity? Well, now they can solve the problem. The Big Guns will be looking at the big picture, and they will develop big plans—and propose big solutions.

The composition of the players who make up the Big Guns isn't necessarily their rank within your organisation—it's their perceived value in answering this particular problem. And this is again why it's important that your business has an understanding of the code words you're using: for instance, if you think you're a Big Gun in the business, and you aren't invited to the Big Gun meeting, does that make you are a Little Gun? No, not if you understand the meaning of the code. These Big Guns are simply the best people to solve this *specific* problem. It might include the person who leads your IT division, your HR Director, your Sales Director and so on. It will always include the CEO, or whoever is the leader of the new business drive—putting their name on the line with a BHAG that everyone in the company understands—and who everyone will hold accountable if they fail.

These Big Guns should have the ability, based on their knowledge and intuition, to come up with some possible solutions as set out in the brief and the Swot Team findings. What we're after at this stage isn't the final answer, although it's quite possible to come up with the right answer in this meeting—it's amazing what you can do when you're armed with all the facts. No, the real purpose of getting the Big Guns together is to give you some ideas with which to test the waters.

Right now we want a 'misty picture' of what might be a possible answer. Using the picture analogy to breaking point: it hasn't come into clear focus yet but it looks like it might be a seascape rather than a landscape. Whether it's a modern painting with bright shapes and colours or a Monet masterpiece we don't know yet. What we do believe is that we'll need a seascape to win this pitch. Now we'll stop with the picture analogy.

SOLVING THE PROBLEM, THEN SOLVING THE SOLUTION

We both worked with a man named Ross Quinlivan, one of the greats of advertising on any number of levels—great ad man, great speaker, a wonderful human being. He died way too young back in 1981 from too much scotch and too many cigarettes. A humourist to the end, his self-written headstone reads, 'Here lies Ross Quinlivan—he died of everything'. He left a lasting impression on both of us.

One of the great things about Ross was the way he looked at a problem. For example, there was the time he was talking to a client of ours who made margarine. Margarine ads pretty much all looked the same with lots of pictures of mothers concerned for their families and rolling fields of sunflowers.

Anyway, in this heavy meeting talking about yellow fats Ross pulled out a bunch of print ads and said for this particular brand these are the kind of ads and the kind of people you're talking to. And he placed on the table a few ads for perfume.

What connection did perfume ads have with yellow fat? Simply that women could be spoken to in a different, more feminine way—not necessarily just as wives and mothers feeding their family.

And Ross had an expression that we've always liked because it sums up what the Big Guns in this problem-solving meeting have to do. He used to say, 'Solve the problem, then solve the solution'. It sounds stupid, or illogical or ungrammatical, but when you think about it for a moment it's actually not.

The point is that once you know what the problem is, and how to solve it, there are a number of ways of 'solving the solution'. For instance, if you know that the problem will be solved by new technology that reduces costs, you can package that IT idea in a variety of ways that best match your client's needs. It might seem like a strange expression, but solving the problem and then solving the solution is the best way we know to attack the big issues in a presentation or business pitch. The way that the idea is packaged is also usually the best way to solve the real problem as well.

THE ROAD TO THE SOLUTION

To come up with possible solutions after the James Bond debrief, the Big Guns should have enough background material to know the territory where the potential solution might lie. But there are a number of questions the Big Guns need to ask themselves on the road to the solution. Here are those questions, and why they're important.

1. What Do You Know about Them?

Your Swot Team should have given you a clear picture of the business you're pitching to and the players involved. Now you need to ask, what's missing from your knowledge bank? Where are the gaps that need to be filled between now and the pitch day?

You and your team will need to create a list of questions about them and their business that occur to the Big Guns based on the knowledge they've been given in the James Bond debrief. Once those questions are formulated you decide what is the best way to discover the answer to those questions.

2. What have We Got that They Want?

You need to know why you are on the pitch list in the first place. What are you well known for? Are you simply there to make up the numbers or is there a simple explanation for your inclusion?

Deciding exactly what it is you have that they want is often the simplest way to get to the best solution. But are you sure it's what they really want? (See chapter 3, 'Bumble'—Why Will They? Why Won't They?)

3. What Inside Knowledge do You Have?

There may be things you know that none of your competitors know. Anything at all might be important, so put it down.

4. Do We Share any Alliances?

Maybe your company shares a supplier with the company you're pitching to. Find out if that's the case and talk to the people you deal with at that supplier. See if you can get them to talk about what it's like to deal with Company A.

- What kind of business do they run?
- Do they have a tight chain of command?
- What are the real business issues and what are the real personal relationships?
- What attitudes do they hold?

Anything you can find out from these shared alliances might give you a clue to the eventual answer. Or, just as good—give you a way of packaging your answer in the most favourable light. Sometimes the solution needs to be presented like a soft-shoe shuffle—nimbly stepping around the political landmines.

5. Do We Have an Existing Relationship?

You need to take a close look at the people who make up the Key Decision Makers in Company A. Are there any individuals there that the Big Guns know personally? Are there any of their friends you might know?

You're looking for ways to better understand the people you'll be talking to. The best way to do that is by knowing them as well as you can. Ask yourself, are there any business associates of yours who might know them, and what could they give you in the way of information that might help in the packaging of your solution?

6. Can We Draw on Previous Experiences?

You need to find out if the problem you're looking at reminds any of the Big Guns of similar situations in the past.

- How was that problem solved?
- Equally, has this client had this problem out to pitch in the past?
- Do they regularly review this area of the business and assign the contract on the basis of regular reviews? In that case, what do

you think was the winning strategy for the last successful pitch?
- What was the one thing Company A was looking for back then?
- How have things changed since then?
- Has management changed and if so, does that mean that everything decided by the old management was ipso facto wrong?

'Not invented here' (that is, the solution they have now was inherited by them from a previous management group) is a very powerful lever, and if you know that you can use it for all you're worth. Out with the old in with the new! (You!)

7. What's Coming Down the Pipeline?

There may be things in your business coming down the pipeline that will be of great interest to Company A that at this point only the Big Guns may know about—some new methodology that will allow you to do things better and more efficiently, or that will deliver much more measurable degrees of success.
- Just as importantly, do you know what's coming down the pipeline of Company A?
- Do they have overseas owners who want to push through a certain way of operating?
- Do they have a new production plant that's coming on line, and if so how will this impact upon the problem they've posed and the best way for you to solve that problem?
- Is their marketplace changing and if so what are the key drivers of those changes?
- Is the prospect an agent or a victim of that change?

8. What are the Big Guns' Intuition on the Real Issues?

When you have as much information as you can gather from this meeting—which is to say, enough to have a snapshot of the company, but not enough for an X-ray—what do you think the real issues are? If you like, at this point you can think of yourselves as doctors looking at the patient in the surgery. You've heard what they've had to say for themselves (the brief), you've done a cursory examination of all the fundamentals (the Swot Team) and you can have a stab at the diagnosis.

What you haven't done yet is go through the full battery of tests, to find out what the real problem is. But you can still look at your patient, in this case Company A, and have a pretty good idea of what the matter is. Your 'misty picture' solution is the path to the cure.

9. What do We Think our Competitors will do?

One of the key questions that needs to be addressed is what you think your competitors are going to do when they are faced with the same set of problems that Company A have outlined in their brief. Sometimes it's not even possible to know who your competitors are, but there are ways of finding out. If you do know who you're up against, you need to look at them closely.

- What are their strengths?
- What are they likely to do to win this pitch?
- What are they famous for? Is it customer service, or great technology solutions or is it a key individual who's seen as a star and might be the one big difference between your pitch and theirs?

You need to think these things through carefully because, as we've said, winning isn't just about providing the best solution—sometimes it's hard for the prospect to judge what's 'best'—it's about making sure everyone else finishes behind you by such a margin that there is daylight between you in first place and those who are second. And there are ways to do that—some of them a bit crafty. But hey, this is war right?

10. What are our Competitors' Achilles Heels?

Just as you've gone through the likely strengths of your competitors, it's equally important to look at the things that could bring them down. Are they too big to handle this business personally? Are they weak in certain areas you think are important?

Go through all the possible negatives and begin to list them—put those negatives alongside the names of your competitors. You're going to use that knowledge to your advantage in the presentation.

By now we trust you're getting the impression that in winning business there is a lot more involved than just turning up on the day with a neat solution presented eloquently. It's at this point in the nine steps that a vital question needs to be asked ...

DO WE REALLY WANT THIS BUSINESS?

So now you know we're nuts, right? 'Of course we want the bloody business, why have we just spent between two and five days of our precious time getting the Swot Team to do all their work and then spent another few hours talking about the possible solutions if we didn't want the damn thing!?' Fair enough. But now that you know a lot more about Company A than you did at the start of the process, do you really want to work with these people?

- Have you gained any kind of impression of the way they do business?
- Are you impressed with the quality of the people in Company A who you will be dealing with, perhaps on a daily basis?
- Do they strike you as being honourable, with rich integrity?
- Do they have a record of paying on time, are their financial affairs above board?
- Are their terms reasonable and acceptable?
- Will you be rewarded for success?

It's easy to fall into the trap of believing that every new opportunity to make a buck for your business is more than likely a good thing. But it's our experience that the wrong company can infect your own business with a lot of negative energy. No matter how big the prize, you have to be certain that it's worth the wear of winning. Your culture within your business is precious (or should be), and it's quite remarkable how one bad client can create a malaise right through your people.

It comes down to the simple question—do you want to work for these people? Sometimes no amount of revenue is worth the pain that a bad client can inflict on the rest of your business. Don't be like some winning bidders at auctions where the desire to win exceeds the value of the purchase.

Are They Pond Scum?

Frederick F. Reichheld, in *The Loyalty Effect* (Boston, Mass: Harvard Business School Press, 2001), refers to those clients who are continually troublesome as 'Pond Scum'. He draws the analogy of fishing in his boat on the lake near his home. He starts in deep water in the centre because that's where the big fish are. But as he has no luck he eventually moves into the shallows where the little fish are, because he doesn't want to go home empty handed. 'A fish is a fish.' 'A customer is a customer.' Wrong.

As he gets into the shallows looking for any fish he can find, the outboard starts to stir up the pond scum on the lake floor. It gets into the engine, clogs up the system and now he's cast adrift on the lake. He has to hail a passing boat to give him a tow and his boat is in the workshop for a week at a cost of $1000—all because he was desperate for a fish. Be selective with the clients you go fishing for. The bad ones will clog up your system and cost you more than they're worth.

Now that you've done a little thinking about whether you want to work with these people, ask yourself this question ...

How Big is the Prize?

Quite remarkably, many companies go into a business pitch without knowing precisely what they're going to win. The revenue may be attractive, but what it will deliver in profit is the real test of how much you should invest in the pitch, if at all.

They might know what it is they're aiming to win—a contract, a supply deal, a big new account. But they don't bother to quantify the actual cash that will flow to the bottom line.

The very best kind of wins are those where you add revenue that goes straight to the bottom line and no extra costs. But those kinds of wins are all too rare. More often than not a new contract will require an investment on behalf of your company. It could be in new staffing, new technology upgrades—in fact any number of things that add to the overhead of your business.

When you look at the prize, is it sufficiently big enough to be worth the effort?

HOW MUCH DO YOU WANT TO INVEST?

It may be that the prize is big enough to be worth a large investment in hours and capital. It could be the kind of win that galvanises your business, or changes the shape of your business, or the way your business is seen by your competitors and possible new clients.

But at some point you have to have a budget, and stick to it. So what is that budget, and can you afford it? If this was a capex request for a piece of equipment it would have a detailed assessment of options, benefits and expected 'return on investment'. Why should this be treated with any less respect for shareholders' interests?

Once you've calculated the size of the prize and the odds of winning, you're better positioned to determine how much to bet. It has to make compelling business sense, and you have to make the decision, yes or no? No? Then politely decline the invitation and thank Company A for thinking of you. Yes? Then there's only one more thing you have to do—decide to win!

John Bertrand Decides to Win the America's Cup

John Bertrand is a great Australian, as well as being a great Australian sporting hero. We're both fortunate enough to call John a friend. He and his wife Raisa are wonderful company. But one thing you need to know about John—he wants to win. He's bloody relentless.

No better example of this can be found than at Newport, Rhode Island in September 1983. *Australia II*, the yacht with the Ben Lexen winged keel, was up against Dennis Conner's *Stars and Stripes*. As every Australian knows the end of the story was a happy one (for Australia)—after the Americans had held the America's Cup for 132 years, John and Alan Bond and a handpicked team of great sailors did what was considered the impossible and stole the Cup away.

We once asked John how he felt when they were one to three down in a best of seven final. Was he worried that all looked hopeless? Was he concerned that if they lost just one more race it would all be over? How would he feel having to front the media as yet another loser in the long succession of losers over the 132 years who preceded him? Was he concerned what his family would think should they lose tomorrow's race, all the years of training and the opportunity cost—both financial and familial? The hopes of a nation were riding on him and his team. Was he starting to prep his excuses?

He looked at us genuinely puzzled and asked what we were talking about. It was as though we were speaking in a foreign language and he said, 'I can honestly say that the thought that we might lose never once entered my mind'. As John describes it, they never had any doubt that they would win, because they had already as a team 'decided they would win!' They rehearsed over and over in their minds what it was going to be like for the first time in their lives to be sailing in front of the 'red boat'. They didn't even dignify their competitor with a name. They saw themselves always in front and made themselves comfortable in that space, rather than freaked out because, until now, the US had always been in front.

You need to make a decision at a moment in time that you are going to win—not just compete—and leave the decision to the judges. Decide that you and your team will do everything that you need to do to win. Decide it together and form a band of brothers who'll go into this battle shoulder to shoulder with no daylight in between.

Of course John came back from one to three down to win the last three races and sail into America's Cup history.

breathe

{ step 3. bumble }

understanding their people

'You can tell a lot about a fellow's character by his way of eating jellybeans.'
Ronald Reagan

Now we need to delve deeply into all the issues involving those people who will be making the decision at Company A. The task for the Pitch Leader at this point (in consultation with the Big Guns) is to find out as much as possible about your audience on the big day. The aim of understanding your audience is simple—you want every vote, and you want every discussion that those Decision Makers have to be positive about you and your business solution. Because this isn't a popular election and because businesses don't work like democracies, you won't win just by aiming for a simple majority of votes—you will only win if you aim to get every single vote.

The analogy to think of is jury selection. Who are the kinds of people who are most like to identify with you? How can you understand them so that they give you their winning verdict? What needs to happen to make them change their minds if they aren't on your side right now? You need to find out because you can't go into this presentation ignorant about the people who will ultimately judge you.

That means that you have to give every single person in the process unassailable, concrete reasons why they should vote for you. And the good news is you can. Because unlike electing a government—where the voters pick the person or the party that they feel most comfortable with based on the broad policies on offer—in your case you can tailor your policy for each *individual* voter. But you can only do that if you know enough about them, and how they work together. The best way of doing that is to meet them, ask them lots of questions and listen intently. Or, if you can't meet them, you must find out as best you can what makes them tick, what is important to them.

You must give each member of the judging panel something tangible and rational as a reason why they should support you. Plus, you must tap into the intangible and emotional issues that will compel them to give a verdict in your favour. To win you need to answer the following questions.

- Who are the Key Decision Makers?
- Who are the influencers on the Key Decision Makers?
- What are all their business needs?
- What are they measured by, what are their KPIs?
- What are their personal needs?
- How will we satisfy their emotional needs?
- What questions need answering, and who is best to ask them?

After you've done all that you should have a crystal clear profile of each member of your audience. You will then craft your presentation so that every single person in that room thinks something like this:

'They understand me, they understand my problems, they know how I work, they know what's important to me, and they know how to solve not just the problem we've set them, but my problems as well!

'Their solution not only solves the brief, they understand our broader strategic objectives and how they are impacted by the solutions they've proposed to this part of the puzzle. I like their style, their manner, I love these people! I can't wait to work with them!'

Now all that may seem like a big ask, and it does require a great deal of thinking, listening and sheer hard work. (And not a little bit of subtlety and cunning.) But it can be done.

WHO ARE THESE PEOPLE?

The first thing you do in your war room is put up a picture (if you have them) of each of the judges you know will be there on the day.

How do you find out who will be there? Well, you can simply ask. There will usually be someone who is the Gatekeeper of the process on Company A's side of the fence. They're responsible for making sure everything is 'fair and above board'. Sometimes you can get the answer directly from them. Sometimes.

You could ring them and be as direct as you can be by asking who will be in the presentation and who will be making the decision. This means that you'll either be lucky and get the information you need or you will be told that the process is confidential and that there will be five people in the meeting including the CEO, or whatever the Gatekeeper thinks sounds like the best answer for you.

In other words, they may be helpful, they may be unhelpful or they may be downright rude. So what do you do now, since, even if you have been given their names, you still don't know the answer to your first and fundamental question: 'What are these people really like?'

This step may well be your first lesson—to really know who their people are you're going to have to meet them. And the first person you have to meet is the Gatekeeper.

No one ever has a relationship until you've shaken hands, or met face to face. Therefore, you need to have a good reason why you must meet them personally. The Gatekeeper needs to feel comfortable with this, because, after all, it's their job to make sure everything is fair and above board. So you acknowledge that when you ring.

We have a rule: we never walk into a pitch and say to someone, 'Nice to meet you'. It's always 'Nice to see you again'. We insist that we meet everyone before the presentation so we can understand their version of what the company needs. We tell the Gatekeeper that's our rule, and point out the benefit to the judges that the ten minutes we spend beforehand ensures that we only spend time addressing the issues that are important to those in the pitch. It shows how we value their time.

Now you have to find a compelling reason to meet the Gatekeeper for a quick ten minutes at their convenience. The best way of getting this time in their diary is to underscore the importance of this pitch. You want to make certain no valuable time is wasted during your presentation, so therefore you'd like some clarification of some points in the brief. (You can always find something that needs more clarity.)

What this does is underline the importance of the Gatekeeper, which should be gratifying for them to hear. And as you make clear, you are not seeking an advantage, you are seeking understanding so that you don't waste anyone's precious time. The wasting of time, and the importance of being on brief are the prime levers to use to get the Gatekeeper to give you some face time. You explain that it's vital that no one from their side feels as though their time is wasted, and it would greatly help the process if the Gatekeeper could give you some time to run through some points that may be raised on the day.

It's possible that the Gatekeeper will say, 'But I can't do that, that's giving you an advantage, surely?'

To which you answer, 'Well, you understand why we want to do this—to ensure we waste no one's time. We also understand that if any of our competitors were to ask you this it would show you were dealing with professional people who wish to do a professional job. So naturally we expect no favours, please do the same for them as you do for us … however, if our competitors aren't quite so thoughtful of your Key Decision Makers' time, well then, that's their fault. We shouldn't be penalised for being thoughtful, should we?' Nine out of ten times you'll get the face time. The tenth time? Ah, we'll get to that.

THE GATEKEEPER'S KEY

Let's say that you've got time with the Gatekeeper. In almost all cases in our experience the Gatekeeper will give you that time. Why? First, because you have given them a plausible reason—clarification of an agenda item, a timing issue, something that needs a point of view from their side, whatever. Secondly, because the Gatekeeper is a human being, and speaking to them as the important person they are validates their role and reinforces their own self-image as someone who is in control of the process.

It's very rare for a Gatekeeper to be impregnable. It does happen that one time in ten or so, but it is very much the exception. When you meet, your aim is to create an ally. That means you wish to create an impression that you are both on the same side. You do this with empathy and with understanding. You also must do it with integrity, because this isn't just play-acting—you really do want to be on their side. To create this feeling of credibility requires that you be as fair-minded with the Gatekeeper as possible.

You must reassure them that you are playing to the rules that they have set. At this first meeting your ethics are paramount. And that's fortunate because you are on very strong ground—you really do want to make this a relevant and powerful presentation, and you really do want to ensure Company A gets the very best out of your business, so that the very best solution is offered.

What you don't do is act as if you are trying to create a friend behind enemy lines. You don't ask, however obliquely, for information that may compromise the Gatekeeper's role—for instance, whether they could tell you who else is in the pitch, or who are the really important votes on the judging panel. This isn't because you don't want to know this of course, you very definitely do—but you don't want to ask too much of the Gatekeeper. Besides, there are other ways of finding out that information.

So your meeting with the Gatekeeper gives you a chance to find out a bit more about them. That's right, you aren't meeting them just to find out about the things on your list of questions, you're there to find out about them personally.

- What are they like?
- Are they a senior player or just playing a role of facilitator for this particular exercise? What influence do they have, if any?
- What do they normally do day to day?

This is a bit like a first date—it's not a blind date, since you've already been introduced, but it is a first date and you want to meet again, get to know them a little better, and better still, get to meet their family. And in this case of course, the family is the panel of judges who will make the decision on the big day.

So the rules of first dates apply. Talk about them, listen intently, and ask questions based upon what was just said rather than the list of topics in your head; generally make them feel comfortable. But just as with any first date, have the sense to know when you're going too far, when you are nudging the boundaries of what is proper and courteous. Be thoughtful, and leave before you're thrown out. Then write to them immediately you're back in the office. This says you're courteous, highly efficient and very interested in their business. Thank them for their time and what they've been able to help with. Give specific feedback if you can.

Now you may be asking yourself: 'What have I got from the meeting?' Well, if you have played your role correctly—with understanding, thoughtfulness, empathy and active listening—you will now have a very much clearer picture of:

1. Who will be in your audience
2. What interests them (from the Gatekeeper's perspective of course)
3. What the pecking order is (again from the Gatekeeper's point of view—it may not be right)
4. What kind of questions to ask the judges.

You report all this back to the Pitch Leader. If you have achieved this, you have an ally on the other side of the fence.

WE'VE COME TO THAT

In that one in ten situation where the Gatekeeper is unable to see you, for whatever reason, you can do one of two things. You can find out a little bit about them, and get to them by other means—through an associate, a friend, an adviser or a mentor—and through these third parties have your case presented for appraisal. Or you can simply accept the fact that the Gatekeeper is keeping the key to the lock (at this stage) and go over the wall, rather than through the gate.

This doesn't mean that you ignore the Gatekeeper. In fact, you will have said in your phone conversation (since you wouldn't have met face to face, otherwise you would have achieved your objective) that you will be trying to arrange meetings with those people who can help solve the problem, at their company. They may very well say, 'They won't talk to you, we won't allow it', but at least you've told them what you intend to do—you've acted correctly and with integrity—and so have they. So, if indeed you do get to talk to those people, it has obviously gone beyond the Gatekeeper; they've done their job and you've done yours.

REMEMBER THE KEY DECISION MAKER

Thanks to your Gatekeeper, and your intelligence network or through a range of other means (such as previous history and the media), you now know who will be in the pitch on their side: these people are the Decision Makers.

Now you need to understand some fundamental points about the Decision Makers on the judging panel that will influence everything else that you do and say, in and out of the pitch.

The first consideration is, who will be the Key Decision Maker? There's always one person with the final say in all this. Often it will be the CEO or Managing Partner; they don't always get their hands dirty sitting on judging panels looking at pitches, they just approve (or make) the final decision.

The problem is that they may not be in the meeting, so they won't see your presentation. They may simply be given a recommendation from the judges and take it, or ask enough hard questions to alter the vote either in your favour or away from you to your (until then) losing competitor.

Let's face facts. No matter what you do, there may be occasions where you simply can't win—due to nepotism, old mates, old obligations, or something dark and mysterious. Worse, there may be times when you won't know any of this. On the other hand, there will be times when you are aware that the ultimate decision will be affected by things outside your control. You can therefore decide whether to pull the plug and save the effort, or use that knowledge to your advantage.

If you decide to go ahead, your aim is to give Company A a solution so plausible, concrete and correct that the recommendation to the Key Decision Maker (who isn't in the meeting) is irrefutable. And that solution will also underscore your knowledge of what that Key Decision Maker also wants.

You will see how that will be achieved as we go through the processes in the following chapters.

Next you need to find out what's important to all the people on the judging panel. You can get some of this by simply reading annual reports, or speeches they've given. Much of this obvious stuff will also have been delivered to you by the Swot Team in their presentation. Those relevant points and areas of interest—relevant to the problem—will be placed underneath the picture (or the name if you haven't got a picture) of that person in your war room. But this is only half the story, maybe less.

The Eleven Key Questions

The best way to understand what these people really want is to get to know them. Having spoken with the Gatekeeper you now have permission to talk to them. You want to meet them face to face. You want to find out what really motivates them. What will compel them to give you their vote? Therefore, your next task is to work out what questions need answering and who is best to ask them?

The questions need to be clear enough to give you an insight into how they see the following things.

1. What is their role in the business?
2. How is their success measured?
3. How will your solution help their role in the business?
4. How do they interact with the other members of the judging panel?
5. How can their own goals be achieved by delivering the solution for the company?
6. How does the solution reward them as individuals?

7. How does the solution recognise their role?
8. How does the solution recognise their values, goals and personal needs?
9. What is the one big thing that will help solve their problems day to day, which your solution can deliver?
10. What do you think motivates them, what are the dominant need states in their life—significance, certainty, variety, contribution, growth or love?
11. Finally, what's the single biggest problem they face?

That's a lot to find out, isn't it? And you won't be able to do it by simply listing those questions and sending the list to them by post. No, this is going to require the right kind of person asking the right kind of questions—listening intently and discovering, by evidence or intuition, precisely what those answers are. But at least you know what the questions are now. How you ask them is an art worth learning, which we'll help you with. But first ...

The Time and Place Rule

This rule applies to all the meetings you have with all the Decision Makers you are hoping to see, including the Gatekeeper—you allow them to set the time of the meeting. This illustrates the supreme importance that you place upon their time—your diary is theirs to use as they see fit. Equally, make certain they know that you also care about your other clients, the ones you have now. You don't want to give the impression that your current clients are taking second place to a prospect.

You can achieve this by mentioning when you meet them at the time they've suggested that your current clients' needs are being looked after. This endorses your thoughtfulness and also shows that in this exercise your current clients aren't the losers. You and your team are simply working harder, because you really need this business.

So the meeting happens at a time of their choosing. However, it may be that the place of the meeting can be used to your advantage. Again, this point doesn't just apply to the meeting with the Gatekeeper—this applies to all meetings you have with Company A's Decision Makers.

You may wish to have the meeting at your offices. Why? To show the substance, scale or culture of your business, or to show some aspect of it that you know is relevant to the person you're meeting with. Think about the content of the meeting and its context.

They may not feel comfortable going to your place. That's understandable and not a problem. Go wherever they feel comfortable. But if you really want them to see your business, then try and arrange that (and have a great reason worked out) at your initial meeting at their place.

Who are the Influencers?

The Influencers are people who don't actually have a vote, but can influence those who do. It's surprising who these influencers might be, and even more surprising what they are influenced by. The most obvious group are those people who simply work with the judges. They are part of the team, but don't have any say in the final decision. Therefore, you need to remember one of the key rules of leadership—treat everyone equally. How you act with them, how you treat them all will affect how they feel about you for good or ill.

Never forget that everyone is influenced by their team mates. If they sense that you or your business aren't treating their mates correctly, they will make you pay.

The more obvious influencers are the people you discover are the mentors, associates or friends of the Decision Makers. It's obviously not possible to get to all of these people, nor would you want to. However, you may discover during the course of your enquiries that a particular person has a special 'issue'. It doesn't really matter what it is, but for the sake of this let's say it's that they worry that your business is too big: 'I'm worried that we won't get their attention because they have so many other clients'. Because they feel that way, you can obviously address that in the course of the presentation. Or you may choose to address it by taking it up with an influencer before the presentation. Hopefully you will know an associate, a mentor or an ex-employer of the person with the issue. The task here is to get that influencer to rebut the objection—in this case, the 'too big' problem. The best way of doing this is to give the influencer evidence that can be used to help make your case that you aren't too big— evidence based on facts, or their own personal experience. How the subject is broached depends upon the circumstances—it could in fact be part of your presentation, or it could be done with subtlety. You have to decide the best method.

Finally, while there are people who may not be able to influence the judging panel, they can still help influence the result—in your favour. These people are as obvious as the PA of the Gatekeeper to the less obvious, such as the person who runs Company A's garage or the night watchman.

There are no Little People

You know yourself that there are individuals who treat people 'beneath them' with contempt, or perhaps with a simple lack of regard. People like that wouldn't benefit from the following two nice stories that happened to us.

In the first instance, we were very anxious to be the last team to present in a six-way new business pitch. By the end of the first week we had gotten to know the PA of the woman who ran the show. We'd treated the PA with respect and had generally got along well, on an equal footing. We knew that every other agency pitching wanted to be last, because in this particular case it was the best place to stand out (although not always, and we'll explain why later). So we figured that this PA would be bombarded with people ringing her up, imploring her, bullying her, bullshitting her and generally schmoozing her, just so that they could wangle their way into her heart, and into the position they wanted—that is, last.

So all we did was tell her, 'Mary, we know everyone is going to be after a particular spot on the pitch list, first, last or wherever.

Therefore, we want to make it easy for you. We'll go wherever you want us to go, it really doesn't matter to us'. And frankly we meant it. But because we'd understood her difficult position, and empathised with her, she just asked, 'Where would you like to go, if you had a choice?' And we ended up in the best spot. Pitched last, but came first. We sent her flowers to thank her afterwards too.

Another time we were reconnoitring a presentation venue, and in this case we were first on in the morning. Over the course of several visits to the site we'd met the guy who was the night watchman. Typical night watchman—the sort of person who has a little bit of power, and can use it for good or ill. In this case, it was actually spending the time to get to know him that allowed us to 'break the rules' and get into the building after hours, to set up the presentation room our way.

We treated him with respect, were genuinely interested in his story, and would have understood completely if he couldn't comply with our wish. But if you treat people as equals, they will reward you (almost always) and you can benefit from their friendship.

Again, even though in that case we didn't win the business, we still sent the bloke a case of beer as thanks—because he did go out of his way to help (and you never know when you might be pitching the account again).

VE VILL ASK DER QUESTIONS!

Have you noticed how the best interviewers—people like Michael Parkinson or Barbara Walters—don't have a long list of questions that they refer to? Rather they have broad themes they want to explore (if their subject will let them) and, most importantly, they ask questions based on what was previously said, which lead on from the last point or a point made earlier. Opposite to that is the kind of brusque interrogation where the interviewee is subjected to a barrage of questions that are rattled off, answered without really being listened to, and the really interesting avenues are ignored in pursuit of every question being asked.

You know which is best to watch, and you also know which would be best to face, if you were being interviewed. The difference is that the best interviewers are very active listeners—they listen, they don't wait for a pause to ask the next question. The best interviewers follow the threads of the conversation, and the astonishing thing is the places such active listening takes you!

Just as there have been occasions where these famous interviewers have had their guests reveal on camera quite remarkable intimacies, so too with the people you will be interviewing. (Although perhaps 'interviewing' is too strong a word, maybe 'chatting with' is closer to the style we're after.) But this kind of intimacy will only happen if they trust you completely, and that requires that you are as interested and as involved in what they are saying as you can possibly be. This can only take place if your goal is to understand them. It won't happen if you have questions that they need to answer. Understanding them will deliver you the answers you want. Simply asking questions may lead you down blind alleys.

WHAT WILL YOU DISCOVER?

If you refer back to the Eleven Key Questions on pages 67–8 you see that few of them can be answered with a direct question. Most of those eleven questions are very much about the inner thoughts and feelings of those people who will be making the decision. And many of them are laden with so much import that it would be impossible to ask them anyway, at least directly—'How do you get on with your MD?' isn't a question you're likely to get a straight answer to. But what will happen is that you will begin to build a portrait of this person, based upon not just what they say, but how they say it, even the way they act as they talk to you.

There are, however, several questions among those 'Big 11' that can be asked quite directly, because they relate straight back to the issue you are discussing—solving the problem set out in your brief. Obviously they know that you are looking for clues as to where they think the answer might be found. And they will either be willing or unwilling to share those views.

In your earlier sessions, where you took a stab at solving the problem, you should have formulated an idea where the possible answer would be found. So this foreknowledge can guide you during your discussions. Remember though, at this point you haven't solved the problem—you are still investigating areas of possibility. But what you are doing is discovering how these possible answers might affect the person you are talking to.

One of the ways of discovering this is by asking one of the few questions you are freely permitted to ask, and that is: 'What is your role in the business?' What you are really asking is 'what's your definition of success in your job?' You need to get as clear a picture of their role as you possibly can. Ask questions that require a bit of thinking—you want to explore all the avenues that open up. Keep following the tracks that a question as straightforward as 'Tell me about your role?' will take you.

You want to begin building a picture of what matters to this person— what things inside and outside the business affect the success of their role in Company A's business? You'll start to see things through their eyes, and of course that is the key to winning their vote—by seeing how the answer will help them succeed in their job, as well as answer the specific problem outlined in the brief.

You might also find it possible to ask this question: 'What is your success measured by?' Most people won't have too many issues with that because it seems a fairly obvious question. However, what you learn from the answer will be vital to getting their vote on judgment day.

If you know that they are rewarded for an increase in sales volume rather than profit then you can have part of the presentation which will allow them to see how your answer directly solves both the problem, and their own problem—increasing sales volume. It's this congruency—the ability for each Decision Maker to see how they will personally benefit from your solution—that will gain you their vote. The only proviso being the obvious one—it has to answer the bigger problem too.

That same thinking—the congruency between their interests and your answer to the problem they've set—will determine your success. If you can create that congruency with everyone, then you are assured of success.

Finally, there is one last question—the Big Question—that you can ask directly, and you can ask it because it is such a big question it seems unlikely that answering it will compromise them or help you specifically. That question is, 'What is the single biggest problem facing (a) you, (b) this company and (c) the industry?' You don't ask the second half of the question—'which our solution can deliver'—because that will be up to you to work out.

Because 'the single biggest problem' is such an interesting question—think about it in your own case—you will most likely find them laughing at the very thought of it. And you will often get humorous answers in response. Listen very carefully to what they say, for it's very true that 'many a true word is spoken in jest'. For instance, the CEO may say, 'Herding cats!' Then your solution should demonstrate how you can help them get buy-in from staff so that everyone is pulling in the same direction.

What they will often tell you is very revealing about the real problems they face day to day. The answer is often fascinating in its revelation of problems inherent in Company A. We've heard people, on being asked 'the big question' give remarkably candid answers, from wanting a simplified approvals process, to complaints about communication systems to numerous personal gripes and irritations.

All of these things should be very carefully noted—because it may be possible to solve their 'one big thing' in the course of your presentation. By the way, ask them if you can take notes as you talk to them. This not only helps in your debrief to the team, but it also demonstrates how important you think their opinions are. Learn the art of actively listening—that means being careful to understand everything they say. Indeed, sometimes it's a great way of getting more information that they may be willing to give, simply by asking a follow-up question that asks for amplification. Or even by simply saying, 'Could you explain what you mean by that?'

KNOWING THEIR SECRETS

As you're talking to them notice what signals they send out in non-verbal ways that give you clues to any areas where they may feel discomfort.

What is your guess as to why they feel that way? Is it because they feel powerless in this area? Is it because they feel the person given the responsibility in that area isn't up to the task? There are endless examples of the 'power of the unsaid'.

You will also find a picture is being built in your mind of the kind of person you're talking to. You do this every day anyway, so this shouldn't be a stretch—but you need to be very aware of what's going on as you talk. Is this person open and forthcoming, friendly and outgoing or are they the opposite? They may simply be on the defensive, not willing to give you too much for fear of compromising themselves or the process. On the other hand, they may also give you directly false information, designed to confuse you and poison your solution. That kind of behaviour fortunately happens rarely, but it does happen. The only defence against it is to see whether the other interviews that have been conducted, or the other investigations you and the Swot Team have carried out, support what this person is saying.

You may find that their surroundings tell you something about them. Are there photos on their desk? What trophies are displayed? Is there a sense that this individual enjoys team environments or are they someone who's more at home in a trout stream in quiet contemplation?

Do you get a sense from their office that they're a good team leader (if they are a leader), and do you get the feeling from the office vibe whether this person is a disciplinarian or a more relaxed and convivial player?

All of these things won't necessarily help you solve the problem. But what they will do is give you a better understanding of how to frame the solution to suit this particular judge.

Finally, what is your impression—from all the things you now know from what you've seen and heard—about what drives them on? There are six possible answers, which we refer to as the 'Emotional Need States'.

There are six emotional need states (whether you like it or not we all have them to a greater or lesser extent within us). We happily credit Anthony Robbins as the person who may have invented this list—at least he's the person we heard it from. They are significance, certainty, variety, contribution, growth and love. At varying times in our lives they change emphasis, and they are in a constant state of flux. The defining thing about them is that they have a prime importance in the way we see ourselves, and in turn how the world sees us. They are in different combinations and to different degrees craved by everyone. If you can identify the greatest need states of the judges, then you can fashion the business solution and deliver it in a fashion that matches these emotional needs.

Significance

This is our need to be recognised for who and what we are. It's what drives people to want titles and corner offices and cars with famous emblems on them. But that's the shallow side of significance (sorry).

The deeper side of significance is the way people react to you and the job you do. One of the chief causes of marital disharmony is the inability of either or both parties to reward the other with a recognition of their significance in the marriage. The cry of 'you take me for granted' is an exact reflection of what significance is all about.

That same lack of regard can happen in business too. At various times we've all felt taken for granted. We all know the feeling that we are having our abilities overlooked. It's frustrating. And it leads to people growing sullen and uncommunicative, or the opposite and flying off the handle—and let's face it, neither is a good look.

So look at those people you're talking to. Do they feel they are being taken for granted? Is gaining a feeling of significance important for them? Well, we can fix that in our presentation, can't we? Build into the presentation recognition of how important that person is to the company, to the process, and to the solution. Show them how embracing you and your solution will elevate their own importance.

Certainty

Certainty is a corollary of confidence. It's the search for certainty that sometimes impels people to fear commitment: 'I don't know if I can trust him, I don't know if he's right for me'. In business that need for certainty can lead to indecision—that's because the indecision is a function of a lack of confidence.

In presentations you will have already discovered that some people don't need to have certainty, they will trust their instincts or the instincts of others to lead them to the right conclusion. Equally (and just as validly) there are others who need to be convinced with evidence before they give you their confidence. That means that it's very important for you to know who among the Decision Makers are looking for certainty, and who rely more on gut instincts (or the instincts of others).

Certainty can only be delivered by proof and evidence. Therefore, where you are dealing with someone who is looking for certainty, you must support your arguments with proof—credible evidence that this answer is the right one. Then and only then will those people have the confidence to give you their vote. Back your recommendations with case studies, research, testimonials, anything that gives the client further evidence that this is a bullet-proof solution.

Variety

There are many people who like living their life in an orderly pattern. The classic stereotype is of the uniformed British clerk—bowler-hatted and umbrella-ed on the 8.10 to Kensington Station. You might therefore suppose that variety is the opposite of certainty. Well, that's not quite so.

Variety is the search for excitement or, if you wish for a word less provocative than 'excitement', then let's try 'interest'. Many people choose their jobs based upon a certain skill set, only to discover that the job is very closely defined. They seek variety by looking for other ways of using those skills. Or they leave that career for a different one where there is inherently more variety. Many CEOs tend to seek variety, the ability to delve into many areas of the business while always maintaining a core competency.

You should be able to discover whether the people you speak to are looking for variety by the way they act and the way they talk. Even from their office if you get a chance to see it. Look for clues that tell you that they are interested in a variety of things, and are looking for 'spikes' of excitement in their life or in their business environment.

People who are seeking variety tend to want to move along in a presentation. They like a lot of ideas and a number of choices. They don't really want to be bogged down in the details for long. Therefore, when you reach the part of the presentation relevant to the judge who you identify as seeking variety, think of ways to make it entertaining, involving and short.

The congruence of certainty/variety is best demonstrated in the format of the classic *Tonight*-style shows on American TV. We have our certainty satisfied because we know the host and the format. The entry, the stand-up, the musical sting and the final sit-down at the desk, even the regular segments—all those things we know and they give us certainty. Variety comes from the guests and the nature of the interviews and the surprises inherent in live television.

Contribution

People who seek the feeling of contribution in their lives are looking for involvement. They aren't necessarily looking for recognition (of their contribution)—they're looking for ways to help, and to be seen to be involved in solutions.

We all want to feel that we're contributing to our relationships, the company, our family and the community. People who are 'contributors' tend to be the 'doers'. They want to get things done, and will be very willing to add their point of view or to put their effort in for the good of all. Therefore, these people tend to be more forthcoming when you speak with them. They'll be happy to talk and get involved in the process.

But a word of warning—they can also tend to hijack the process, and your solution, so that their contribution ends up being your solution. Simply because they've put so much effort in, and are so involved that they will be the loudest voice you hear.

The key here is to make sure that the answer you provide allows them to see how their involvement can or has made a difference to the outcome. You will be actively seeking their help in delivering the solution, and you want to make that clear, but again a word of warning—the other judges may not wish to abrogate the responsibility to your keen contributor. Also, they may not be that central to the solution. Even so, make sure that you tell them somehow, someway that their involvement will be vital to the successful implementation of your idea. You may even hint in the presentation to the value this person has already contributed in helping you to understand the needs and how they inspired a thought. That way they will be far more likely to give you their vote, after all, they will be part of the answer!

Growth

Personal growth is a lifelong need for all of us. Sometimes it manifests itself in searching for new career paths, other times it may be as simple as reading a self-help book. We all want to feel that our relationships are growing, that our careers are growing and that we are maturing.

When you think of growth, and the individual involved, think of the destination they are heading towards. It could be as simple as being part of a success, and how that success can influence their career path. It could be more to do with personal growth, linked to a maturing of an attitude or idea. It may be that the two are linked and that the personal growth will deliver career growth by new learnings or new skills. Or by new responsibilities that require a stepping-up to a new level of achievement.

As you talk to your Decision Makers, understand that all of them will be anxious for some kind of growth. Your challenge is to find where the growth is most likely to be in congruence with your solution to their problem. It could be that you will need to challenge them in some way, suggesting that they need to do this, achieve that before an answer is delivered. Those challenges will lead to growth, whether personal or aligned to their career path. Either way, you will win their vote if you can find a way of giving them that opportunity.

Love

This is the biggest need of all and wraps up all the others. What it really means is that we value the individual for who they are. This means that we are thoughtful about their needs and are always thinking of them and how they feel. It translates in the presentation down to the simple courtesies that are so often overlooked—the thoughtfulness of speaking not just to one person but to each and every person in the room. It shows itself in the value that you place upon a response to a question.

Love is the eternal piece of the puzzle that makes people feel good about themselves.

We don't suggest that you blow kisses and send flowers, just remember that love is thoughtfulness and a generosity of spirit that is clearly present in truly great presenters and is absent in the wannabes.

SO WHO'S ASKING?

One of the key questions the Pitch Leader must answer is who will be asking these questions of the Decision Makers? There are two schools of thought. The first is that one individual, who will be highly involved in the solution and will therefore be very involved in the running of the day-to-day business of Company A, does all the interviewing.

There are obvious advantages to this approach. They get a very good picture of the entire business they're dealing with. They become quite visible at Company A. And hopefully they create great relationships with all the main players and Decision Makers. You just have to be very confident that you've picked the right person. Is their chemistry right for Company A? Do they reflect the kind of things and the sorts of values that your business aspires to? Because after all, they will become the face of your business.

The alternative is to have a hand-picked core team, kept to a small number, who meet with the appropriate people, who you have carefully chosen based upon their competencies aligned to their interviewee and the values you wish to reflect for that particular Decision Maker. For instance, if you want to illustrate that you are an energetic youthful business, you might want to think about whether your hand-picked questioner is also youthful and energetic.

You might also want to choose individuals based upon their chemistry. Some people work well with certain types of individuals and some don't. Your task is to decide what is the right fit for each of the Decision Makers.

The profile, age or stature of a Decision Maker within the business could also be a factor. Obviously the CEO will most appreciate talking to a fellow CEO, and so on.

You also need to think about their 'fit' in the business structure. Will the individual feel comfortable knowing that their interviewer is going to be responsible for a particular part of Company A's business which they control?

Whichever way you decide to go, what's vital is that there is a pre-determined method for ensuring all learning is shared with the Big Guns who will solve the problem. That means having the discipline to dump down either on tape or through written notes all the information that's been gathered. That then leads us to the final part of the puzzle ...

THE NICKNAME TRICK

The final part of this journey of discovery, of getting to know them, is the summation. In your war room under each of their names (and pictures) you will now have bullet points that are the answers to the Eleven Key Questions you have asked your judges. Those answers are the key to winning their votes. It's very easy, however, to become distracted from the task of winning each of those votes as you work towards the answer.

Remember that the only way to win is to make sure you win every vote on your way to delivering the solution. That means you have to remember at all times that these Decision Makers are individuals— individuals who you now know more about than your competitors do. And as individuals they each have needs different from and separate to every other Decision Maker.

So how do you guarantee your answer also covers their issues, their job demands and KPIs and embraces their emotional need states? The answer is surprisingly simple. You give them nicknames! Not derogatory ones of course, but nicknames that summarise them and their needs.

You use those nicknames when talking about them, and you check to make sure those nicknames are provided for during the course of your presentation. For example, if Vicki is someone who sees sales volume as the key to success in the market place, then call her 'Volume Vic'. If Sarah, the Company Secretary thinks the share price is the only true indicator of business success, then she becomes 'Share Price Sarah'. If it's clear to you that Henry wants to become famous for doing something great in business, call him 'Hollywood Henry' and so on.

That way you are guaranteed to always be on track—winning their votes one by one, hitting their hot buttons, while solving the bigger problem outlined in the brief. The only caution we can give you is for goodness sake don't call them their nickname in the presentation. 'Easy Life Eddie' might not be that impressed.

ASSIGN ROLE PLAYERS

Now that you know the likely Decision Makers, you need to organise for people in your business to play the role of those individuals when you do your pitch rehearsals. They'll be vital in step eight of our nine steps—'Jump'. You assign people who will 'get into the head' of the people on your jury. Their task is to think like the person they are playing and to consider how the presentation impacts on them. Using the nicknames helps, because it's easier to remember what their hot button is.

One becomes Volume Vic, another Share Price Sarah and so on. They will need to know the buttons that need to be pushed—that's why you've done such detailed profiles. Their task is to be as accurate as they can be in playing that character during rehearsals. They must consider what are the things that are missing that might win the Decision Maker's vote, and what are the hard questions that they might ask? This way your rehearsals will have a reality to them that they might otherwise lack.

We suggest that only the really key Decision Makers are role-played, and that you clearly brief your players so they know exactly how these people might think and react.

breathe

understanding the problem

'Deliberate often, decide once.'
Latin proverb

WHERE ARE YOU NOW?

You've met the people at Company A. This means that you have understood the brief they've given you, but now you've had a chance to get to know the workings of Company A a lot better. By now you should know the kind of business they are in, the people in it, the biggest problems faced by each individual on the judging panel, their company and the industry, as well as many of the inner workings and issues that affect their business.

All of this intelligence allows you to look at their brief from a different perspective. No longer is it a question that is impersonal and formal. Now you know the flesh and blood issues of the business, so you can see the personal relevance of the brief to all of the people who will be making the big decision.

This means that you now can look at the brief from 360 degrees. You know what the brief means to the various people involved. For some, their role is going to be vital in delivering the answer to whoever is the successful bidder/pitcher/tenderer. For others, they will simply be on the jury, but won't have any involvement with you or your solution day to day.

So now you need to tackle the two problems: the problem as outlined in the brief, and the real problem, that may be inherent but unstated. How do you answer both, to win?

HOW THE WORLD WORKS

Why is it that there are so many makes of car? Why does fashion exist? How come we have such a variety of TV to choose from? Well, obviously, that's because we're all different and make different choices and have different tastes. The 'brief' for a car is pretty straightforward, even if it might take a few hundred pages to describe. Even though a Honda answers the brief, you might prefer the Nissan. Why? Because that's the way the world works. The Nissan answers some deeper need than simple transport. It might be looks, it might be your neighbour has one. But whatever—even though both answer the brief titled 'Make Me a Car', you end up buying the one that feels right for you.

The previous section was all about understanding that point from the perspective of your judging panel. Which makes working out what they want a little easier.

FIRST THE BRIEF

Remember at school how the teacher said, 'Read the question carefully'? You have to be sure that you get points for answering the question as outlined in the brief. There are occasions when the brief may be over 120 pages long with subsections and legal issues. Someone, and we recommend the Pitch Manager, has to be responsible for ensuring that every single question has been answered.

Very often these days the tender document or response to the brief is a very elaborate piece of work. And you can be assured that there will be someone at Company A whose job it is to verify that all the questions in the brief have been answered. A surprising number of companies have told us of examples where the brief or document hasn't been correctly answered, or things have been left out or answered hastily.

Nothing must be left to chance, because although we are more concerned with the personal interactions that take place at the face-to-face presentation, you don't want to walk in with a black mark already next to your name because their brief hasn't been answered in detail in your written response. But that doesn't mean you can't answer the real problem as you answer the brief.

THE REAL PROBLEM?

Very often the brief is an exercise in camouflage. As we mentioned earlier, why would Company A put their problems out for all to see? (And yes, even with confidentiality clauses there aren't many occasions when a brief is leak-proof.)

So almost always the brief, whether it's a single sentence or 120 pages, is simply an exercise to see you run through your paces. To find out how hungry you are, to see how you operate, to see if they like your people and to see if there is a cultural fit. Which brings us to the real problem.

Sometimes the real problem is prosaic—'Give it to us cheaper than we're paying now'. Maybe their real problem is cost saving, not low price. Very often though, it runs deeper than that, and very often you will win their business by simply showing them that you in fact do understand what their real problem is.

You might win with a higher price if you can show them how you will change elements of the production or value chain, change their processes or time to market, or how you can take out steps along the way—all resulting in greater profits for them even though your service is not the lowest price.

To understand that problem you need to look at all the intelligence you've gained from all your sources—the Swot Team, media reports, speeches given and last, and most vitally, from your conversations with the main players at Company A. From all this your Big Guns should be able to make an informed decision about what they're really after. Let's call this the 'Problem Defined'.

Problem Defined is a destination that you arrive at through the hearts and minds and KPIs of all the people who are on the judging panel. So it's not a straight line, it has to hit a lot of things along the way. This is why 'Every Child Wins a Prize'—but of course it also has to deliver all the answers as outlined in the brief.

You now have a good idea of the definition of the real problem, and therefore will have thoughts as to what the answer may be and how it will impact each of the judges. But first you must test it.

TAKING THEIR PULSE

Once you've made the decision about these possible solutions to the real problem you've got to do your very best to guarantee it's the kind of answer they're looking for. You do this easily enough— you ask them. Of course we don't mean you give away your secrets. What we mean is you go back to those people you've spoken to and delicately dance around the possible solutions you have.

The best way of doing this is asking questions, such as 'How comfortable would you be with ...', 'Do you think your company needs ...', 'I've got a sense that ...', 'What do you think of ...' and so on—open-ended questions that have plenty of opportunity in them. For example, you may think that the best way to solve the client's problem is to form a joint venture with another supplier who has a specialised edge that—coupled with yours—will provide the perfect solution. But you'd better find a way to test the client's reaction to that answer before you present it. No point walking into the presentation joined at the hip with your new JV partner only to find that the thought of engaging an additional resource is anathema to the prospect, because they've already decided that they'll only consider a provider who can do it all themselves.

If you ask enough questions of as many people as you can from their side, you should get a pretty good feel for whether or not you're on the money. If you continue to find resistance, then keep asking questions until you discover where they feel comfortable with a particular line of inquiry. Then modify your solution to satisfy those concerns.

The earlier you can do this in the process the better, since it gives you more time to clarify and develop your solution. Once you have allies on the client side, use them to help you. Ask for their guidance and give them as many opportunities as possible to point you in the right direction.

All presentations come down to two things—what will be presented and how it will be presented. You've now got the 'What': which is the real problem defined. The next section will show you how to get ideas to solve that problem. Now you must structure the presentation to give you the best chance of winning. That's the 'How'.

solving the problem

'Here's a good rule of thumb. Too clever is dumb.'
Ogden Nash

By now you may be thinking, 'Are these guys nuts? It's taken you until now to get to solving the *@#* problem!?' Well, um, I guess it has.

Now it's true that you can make a good stab at solving the problem as soon as you get handed it. (And you'll notice that's pretty much what we suggest you do.) But with our method you've now pressure-tested that answer; you've found out whether it's in the right area. You also know all the stuff that your opponents won't know to get to the solution that wins the war for your side.

And then there's this—you'll be solving three problems that are being faced—our problem, their stated problem and their unstated problem/s. Their two problems you now understand as clearly as you ever will short of working with them. Our problem is simple—we don't have their business.

UNDERSTANDING OUR PROBLEM

Not having their business is our problem. We now need to deliver to them all the things they want to hear so they will buy from us. Luckily you know this, and you know it much better than anybody else because you've done all the work. So what do they need to hear to give us the business?

What you are looking for at this moment is an answer that looks and sounds right to them—to all of them. It seamlessly solves all the key issues that they have stated (and left unstated) in their brief to you. It doesn't necessarily have to be brilliant, inventive or unique. It just has to hit all the targets set out in the brief as well as those buttons in the heads and hearts of Share Price Sarah, Hollywood Henry and everyone else on the judging panel.

The fact is that not many people can tell a good idea when they see it. If they could, then a lot of great ideas would have been taken up sooner ... electricity for instance, the telephone, radio, television, the personal computer. All of these great ideas weren't grasped immediately and in some cases were actively fought against.

If good ideas were easy to spot, making movies would be a lot simpler. *ET*, for example, was an idea that was picked up by Steven Spielberg after eighteen other producers had knocked back Melissa Mathison's screenplay. He made a bit less than a billion on that one. As William Goldman, the guy who wrote *Butch Cassidy and the Sundance*

Kid, *Marathon Man*, *All the President's Men* and a number of other brilliant stories and screenplays, said about Hollywood: 'Nobody knows anything'.

Even when the evidence is right in front of you, people can still not get it. You reckon if you do a great tap dance on the day of the presentation you'll win through? Okay, what if we gave you Fred Astaire to do the tap dance for you? Now you're brimming with confidence, right?

Bad move. Fred Astaire was given a screen test when he first came to Hollywood, the review of which still exists. Some unknown 'expert' had this to say about Fred and his abilities: 'Fred Astaire: Balding. Can't act. Can't sing. Can dance a little'.

'A little'??!! So go on. Do your tap dance. It isn't going to work because most people don't know how to judge things that they haven't seen before. What you want is an idea that *they can buy*. It may indeed be brilliant, tactically sound and strategically right. But it doesn't have to be. It just has to be bought.

What may stop them from buying it now needs to be addressed. Don't pitch the right answer, pitch the winning answer—that is, solve *our* problem first, we don't have the account. Once we've got it we can solve their problems.

WHY WILL THEY? WHY WON'T THEY?

This is one of the key markers in this whole process, because it gives you the roadmap for your presentation. It can only happen when you have all the information in. So it takes place immediately prior to the solving of the problem and is the foundation for the agenda you will use in your presentation. Here's how it works.

On the whiteboard that you have in your war room, write on one sheet this headline: Why will they? On the next sheet write: Why won't they?

In the room are the Big Guns and all the people who've done the ground work, who've met with the key players and know their issues. You can see right now why all that work was so important, because now you can answer those two questions with a clear-eyed confidence.

Under 'Why will they?' you write down all the things that you know are positives about your business, which this potential client either knows or believes about you and your business. That is, 'Given what they currently think and feel about us, if they had to choose today, why would they give us the business?'

In this category can go all kinds of things that you know are good things. They might include successes you had on similar businesses or similar categories. It might be that you know that some members of your team are viewed very positively by the judges. It could be skills you have. It could be tools that you've revealed to select judges to pique their interest. In other words, this is a cool appraisal of all the positives that you know they know about you, that you want to remind them of in your presentation.

Given the need for brevity in most presentations, if there are some positive qualities that you know they already admire in you, then it may not be necessary to waste valuable presentation time ramming them down their throats. A quick summary of these qualities may be all that's required, thus allowing you to spend time on the areas where they need convincing. But, a word of warning. It can be fatal to assume that every judge has read the brief, read the prior submission materials or is up to speed on all issues. Never assume any of those things. Take the time for a quick recap and ensure you get across the summary of the qualities you think they already see in you.

Once you've spent time thoroughly downloading all those positives, it's time to write down underneath 'Why won't they?' all the reasons (both real and imagined) why they won't give you the business. These issues will be any number of things, from personality-based issues (the toughest ones to mention) right through to your size, your inexperience in the category and so on. Especially important will be any issues that important individuals have raised that may illustrate why they themselves might not vote for you. All those things have to be written down so your team has a clear picture of all the positives and negatives that you face.

All the negatives on the 'Why won't they?' list are obstacles in the way of you getting the business. Now your task is to find a way in the presentation or even before the presentation to address all those issues and maximise the positives and minimise, eliminate or render unimportant the negatives. The goal will be to enter the room with no negatives remaining in the minds of any of the judges, because you'll have found ways directly or indirectly (such as through intermediaries and media articles) to neutralise any negatives.

You can see that only by doing this thorough examination of your chances, and only by knowing all the obstacles in your path, can you give yourselves the best chance of winning. Having written out those points you now know the important points to highlight in your presentation. You now know what needs to be said about you and your business as you solve their problem. Now let's solve that problem.

AN IDEA SOLVES A PROBLEM

This is the best definition of an idea that we know. It may not be the one in the dictionary, but it's the best way to look at what your team is doing now. You have all the information you will ever need.

The problem is, most people don't understand the problem, so they come up with ideas that solve the wrong problem. Which still leaves the problem.

Our methods guarantee that you solve the right problem. In any presentation for any business, whether it's for a large property tender, a large government contract or a prestigious advertising account—you need an idea that separates your offering from anybody else's—an idea that fires their imagination.

To do this you need to think—either collectively or separately. But the thinking has to have a purpose. Therefore, the one thing you need to do, above everything else, is clearly state the problem that your idea will solve. This written statement should neatly encapsulate the key issues of the brief and the unstated problems in the business.

{ the brief }

The brief may be the problem you've been asked to answer, but it may not be the real problem. Very often the real problem is never stated in the brief, but it's still there. The trick is to work out what it might be.

The real problem can be something as simple as the CEO being a new appointment so they've put a rocket up everyone about revisiting all the contracts and partnerships.

Whatever it is, you have to understand that the brief you're working to is probably not the real problem. The trick is to answer the brief you've been given and, at the same time, solve that real problem.

This means being very specific, for example: 'We need to deliver a new management information system (MIS) that will lower costs and directly impact their share price, because margin pressures are rising faster than revenue and market growth. Indirect costs are poorly managed and crippling the bottom line. Their low-share price is impacting their growth because now they can't use scrip for acquisistions'. Their brief may have only asked for the first part, your interviews and hard work would have added the second part of the problem. While that's a pretty straightforward example, it shows the kind of statement that needs to be written out, which your idea will solve.

While your competitors will simply have a stab at the problem outlined in the brief, 'Deliver a new MIS system', your team will know exactly what they need to do to solve that problem and the unstated problem ('Give our share price a spike').

Thomas Edison said, 'There is no length to which a man will not go to avoid the labour of thinking'. It's not easy. But there are methods you can use to help the thinking process. Many of them you would know, from Edward de Bono's 'Six Hats' to simple brainstorming sessions. We have our own patented process we call 'Drilling for Diamonds'. But whatever process you use, the only effective solutions will come from answering the right problem.

SO WHAT'S THE ANSWER?

The answer should be easy to understand. It should be explained in a sentence or two at most. If it's involving an area where few people have a deep understanding (IT is a prime example), it needs to be translated into simple-to-understand English. The reason for this is that someone is going to go with your idea to the Chairman or the CEO of the company you've tendered to, and they're going to say what they think is your answer.

A good example of this is when the company National (now Panasonic) were looking to bring all their products under one big umbrella brand campaign back in the early 1980s. The competitive agency probably had a catchy jingle, clever strap line and a sound strategy. But you can guess how they fared against George Patterson's CEO, Alex Hamill's idea: 'We've bought ABBA as your presenters'. Right when they were the hottest band in the world. Imagine how those two ideas were received when they were presented in Japan. 'We have two ideas to choose from, this jingle, or ABBA.'

If they don't understand it without reading it, then they probably won't give you their vote. And they won't be able to explain it to the top brass if it's too complicated a solution. So your idea needs to have an elegant simplicity to it, no matter how complex it really is, which will allow anyone who explains it to 'get it'. Which means the person they're telling it to will get it as well.

In Hollywood they understand this and they call the process 'High Concept'. Hollywood knows that when you're looking for a green light on a project you really haven't got time to explain the plotting, the twists and the way the photography will really be great. What you have time for is this: 'Schwarzenegger, De Vito: Twins'. Which is a real example (and the shortest ever) of a high concept pitch. You get the idea, in one go. Tall, muscle-bound Arnie and short, fat Danny are twins? Tell me about it? Okay, I will, in a film.

Similarly, the genius of Johnnie Cochran's defence of OJ Simpson was simplicity itself: 'If it [the glove] doesn't fit, you must acquit'. Since it only took 25 minutes to reach the verdict, I bet that line was used a few times in the jury room.

DANGEROUS IDEAS

A number of smart people are credited with the quote, 'Nothing is more dangerous than an idea when it is the only one you have'. It simply means that you need to be very careful about deciding what idea you will be going with. You need to keep drilling until you're certain that you've got the very best answer. Since 'The Good is the Enemy of the Great', you've also got to be very careful about how the process of getting your winning idea is handled. Ideas are fragile things and need to be supported. It's easy to kill good ideas. A frown will do it. But they're a lot harder to get in the first place.

Now is the time for the Pitch Leader to stand up for what they believe. There is probably no more important moment in the whole process than the moment when they say, 'That is the idea we will be presenting'. It's a very lonely decision to make. But fortunately, if everyone on your team understands the various roles, then they will also understand how important it is to have someone make the big decision.

Once it's made it is non-negotiable! Nothing is more important than understanding this simple point. Once you've made the decision, everyone must get behind it. The reason for this is a simple truth that can be clearly observed in successful business: 'He who states his case with the most conviction wins'. They don't necessarily have to be right, but they have to be convinced that they're right. And if they are, then the chances are that they will be able to give a compelling case, sold with great conviction, to support their idea.

Everybody must get behind the idea. If any member of your team tries to undermine it, or doesn't give the idea their support, then they shouldn't be on the team. The time for discussion is past. Once the Pitch Leader has made the decision, then nothing else can arise to change that decision. No backroom conversations. No mumbled disagreements. Everyone must be behind the idea 100 per cent. It doesn't matter if they think they have a better idea, it doesn't matter whether they believe the idea is stupid, or wrong-headed. It only matters that they are behind it.

We've seen and heard examples of indecision that have cost the company who made them dearly. For example, there was a case where a presentation was made and an idea was presented that seemed to have the full backing of the business that presented it. But just after the idea was revealed, a lone voice piped up with another idea, his idea, that he believed was better than the one presented. You can imagine how that went down. Why did he do it? Ego? Courage?

Who knows. What he pitched might have been right—he might have had a better idea—but it was wrong. Because now the client is thinking that these guys aren't on the same team. 'They can't even agree on the idea to present to us.'

This may be an extreme example of the problem, but there is no good that will come from your team members being undecided about the idea that's being presented. This is why it's so important that the Pitch Leader understand the skills of leadership and knows how to make a decision and stick to it.

WHAT AND WHEN

Finally, having worked out the idea that solves the problem, and having done the 'Why will they?' and 'Why won't they?' exercises, the last question to answer is: 'When do we answer these issues?'

You see, what will have happened is that you will have discovered a great number of positives and negatives—more than likely too many to comfortably fit into your presentation timetable. You may also find that some of the issues that have turned up are of interest to only one or two people on the judging panel. Therefore, you need to decide how each of those issues is addressed and you have three choices:

- Before the pitch in a one-on-one meeting, phone call, stage-managed event or through a friendly third party.
- During the presentation itself ... where the bulk of the issues will be addressed, even if only obliquely.
- After the presentation, again with a one-on-one meeting, a letter, a piece of theatre or a phone call.

First know this—if successful presentations are scored out of 100, then this is where the points are divided out:

- Before the presentation you can get about 30 per cent of the points
- 40 per cent of the points are won in the presentation
- 30 per cent are won after the presentation

Therefore it makes sense to use that to your advantage.
- What bits of the presentation will work best one on one?
- Which bits need the drama of the day to get across?
- Which bits can be held back and used as a mighty club at the end?

Study all your issues that need addressing and decide the 'what' and the 'when'. Also, consider the idea that you will be presenting. Does it require any pre-sell? By that we mean, does it require some work before the presentation to get anyone on the judging panel to feel comfortable about this particular direction?

Sometimes all the pre-sell requires is that you forewarn an individual that what they'll be seeing is unexpected, or that the idea that you have may be surprising to them. You then have a chance to involve them in your thinking and get them on your side before the presentation. They will have inside knowledge, and they may well use this inside knowledge to your advantage, with a well-chosen word in the right ear. Or, of course, if you haven't done all your homework they might leak your idea to the other side.

Exactly how they react will be based entirely upon the effort you and your team have put into making that individual feel a part of the process. If you haven't worked out at this stage whether they're for you or against you, then you don't deserve to play on the winning side, and to have a role on the big day. If you know there's a major issue that stacks the odds against you, then our advice is to address it before the meeting. If you can't address it before the meeting then make it item number one on the agenda.

Why? Because if you don't address the elephant in the middle of the room then the client is going to be sitting there listening to your recommendations through their 'yes, but' filter.

Let's share a good example of this. Our Melbourne office had won the account of a national sporting body. They'd had it for over a year when the management of our Melbourne office changed. Soon after we learned that the client had called for a competitive pitch and our office was excluded from the pitch. The two of us had just assumed national roles in the company and thus were now involved in the problem for the first time. Our new Melbourne management tried to get back into the pitch but with no joy. Finally, the client relented and said we could present but it was pretty clear that they wanted nothing more to do with our company and we were a long way behind the eight ball.

We managed to get interviews with most of the clients, but the CEO was adamant that he wouldn't meet with us prior to the pitch. After lots of investigative work and leveraging relationships within the organisation we got to the root of the problem. Our previous management had made a lot of promises to the client when they were pitching for the business over a year before—introductions to major potential sponsors, cross-promotions with some of our other clients and personal commitments of time working on the account, were all paramount in the decision to appoint. But our agency had failed to deliver on these promises.

The CEO felt let down, indeed he thought that our company had lied to him. We then learned that in the earlier meeting to discuss the review and whether we should be invited to repitch, his response at this internal meeting had been a very direct, 'Just fire George Patts!'

So you can see that this information was vital to our approach. No matter what promises we'd be making in the pitch, no matter how good the ideas were, his 'yes, but' filter would be working overtime. He would believe nothing. Every attempt to address it with him prior to the presentation failed.

We had a brilliant advertising campaign developed by one of the finest creative directors Australia has produced, Chris Dewey. We had fantastic promotional ideas and sound marketing strategies for the future. But if it was all to be presented by 'liars' we had no hope of success. When they entered the room you could sense the tension. It was cold as ice.

Ian opened the meeting, not with an agenda or a welcome and introductions but with a single PowerPoint slide that sat silently on screen for fifteen seconds without comment. But for those in the room it felt like fifteen minutes as the discomfort of the words confronted everyone.

The slide read, 'Just fire George Patts', followed by the CEO's name and the date he said it.

Ian said, 'We're here today to present some great marketing recommendations for your business, but it will be pointless sharing them with you if this is the basis of your viewpoint. We are new to this business and have learned that some of our local predecessors made some promises to you that weren't kept. We checked this out and you're right. You were let down and if our roles were reversed, we'd probably arrive at the same statement.

'If you think we're liars then there's little point going on with the presentation because regardless of the quality of thinking, you'll believe we won't deliver. We're new to this account and to this city. And we're people of our word. So we've built in fifteen minutes of our presentation time for you to verify our claim to be people who deliver on their promises. Here is a list of ten CEOs who we've worked with over recent years. Next to their name is the phone number where they can be reached right now. Every one of them is waiting for you to call them and ask the question "are these people of their word?" We know they'll confirm that to you. We'll leave the room now while you make those calls.'

The list included the names of highly regarded CEOs of major telcos, breweries, banks, law firms, airlines, tourism bodies, and food manufacturers, many of whom were known to the CEO. He looked at the list, studied it in detail, then looked up with a broad grin and said, 'Alright, I'm prepared to listen with an open mind, but don't think I won't call them later'. He admired our insightfulness, our willingness to address the tough issues, our competitive streak and our balls for tackling the problem head on. The presentation was brilliant and we won. We delivered on every promise we made and even fulfilled the ones our predecessors had let slip.

breathe

1 3 7

8 2

6

9

5 4

stumble

{ step 4. stumble }

the agenda

'To have his path made clear for him is the aspiration of every human being ...'
Joseph Conrad

Essentially an agenda is a list. It's an *aide-mémoire* to ensure nothing is missed. You can even write an agenda without knowing what the subject is. The Pentagon has a standard agenda it uses before any military operation, and it never changes. In case you're interested here it is:

- Weather
- Intelligence ·
- Operations
- Military Support
- Mobilisation
- Logistics
- Medical
- Public Affairs
- Army Top Concern
- Priorities
- Chaplain

That's it. That covers everything from whether it's raining to making sure the dead are laid to rest with dignity. You can see that a lot of very important stuff is covered by very straightforward language. 'Intelligence' for example, or 'Military Support' could easily be broken down into dozens of component parts. But that's not the purpose of the agenda.

The agenda is there to make sure you haven't missed anything vital, and that things are done in their correct order. The above is the way the US military does it. How do you do yours?

AGENDA, AGENDUMB, AGENDUMBER

How many agendas have you seen in your life? They're usually white bits of paper with a list of things on them. They never look especially interesting, but on the other hand they're handy to have around, because at least you know what's supposed to be happening—even if it isn't happening.

Most agendas are drafted the day of the meeting in a hasty discussion between the main players. Everyone sort of knows their stuff, and there seems to be a relatively straightforward logic to it, so that's the agenda done. Well, really that's an 'Agendumb'.

The pitch agenda should be thought through as carefully as a play. Because in essence a play is what your presentation will be. (We used a movie analogy at the beginning of the book, but now we're dealing with a live audience we'll change our tune.) Think about it. It's got a story to tell, which will be your answer to their brief (encompassing the unspoken issues as well). It has actors, who each play a part—some have leading roles, there may even be a star of the show. There will be bit parts and supporting roles—although there definitely won't be any extras. There is (depending on your answer) drama, humour, understanding, humanity and a resounding climax. There's an audience of course, most of whom you should know by now. It's also (unlike film) totally live. Or completely dead, depending on your point of view and your success or failure. It will also have something, 'The Hook' (and we'll get to that in a moment), which they will remember long after they've left the meeting.

Therefore, the agenda is the central narrative of the play. Everything comes from this piece of paper, and so needs to be carefully thought through. This means that the agenda is written by the Pitch Leader—it's their decision what is said, how it's said, when it is said and by who. Let's look at those four decisions one by one.

THE WHAT

Start with your answer. Your answer needs to be supported by facts and opinions. These facts and opinions comprise a very long list of things that you could say to support your answer. These 'could say' things include all the things that your business could bring to this partnership—the expertise you have in this area, the tools you have. You could talk about the individuals who will be at the meeting on your side—how will they interact with the client? What unique skills do they have? You could address the issues raised in your 'Why will they, why won't they' discussions. You could talk about things you've learned from your interviews.

You now have a complete picture of the business and the people in it (or as complete a picture as you can have, without working with them). The temptation is to show them how much you know and how much work you've done compared to your competitors, so you want to tell them *everything*. But of course you can't. Therefore, the best way of handling this is to write down all those things that you could possibly say, point by point. This exercise allows you to see the complete ambit of your presentation and gives a clear look at the task ahead. You will probably end up with somewhere between ten and two hundred things that you could say.

Now the Pitch Leader's job is to rank those points from one to whatever. They will rank each one based upon what they know to be important to the client, what is vital to the answer itself and what may be vital to individuals on the judging panel. It's important to remember here that each of these points you are ranking won't necessarily play a large part in the presentation. Very often a vital point can be made in an aside, or with something that is outside the confines of the presentation. In other words, it doesn't necessarily have to be covered in the presentation itself to make it an important point to cover.

Also, there's much to be said for a special issue that's of interest to just one of the judging panel being handled separately, outside the presentation—in a phone call, a report, a research item, indeed whatever it takes to drive home the answer to the issue which that individual has.

So now you know what you *could* say, you need to work out what you *should* say. Taking your 'could say' list, your task now is to decide what categories all the things you 'should say' fall into. Every presentation is different so it's impossible to imagine exactly what will be on your 'should say' list, but here's an example of the kind of things you might put together under the column 'Our People':

- Expert knowledge of the category
- Experience with other brands in the market
- Experience with similar problems in other industries
- Overseas experiences
- Particular skill sets
- Honours or achievements that are relevant
- Personal relationships
- Testimonials

As you will see, each of these issues is something that has come from your 'could say' list. Spill them out on a whiteboard at random. They will soon be placed in some kind of order. You will discover that the things that you should say begin to cluster together in a kind of natural order. By the time you've finished your thorough analysis you could have perhaps anywhere from five to twenty headings; underneath each one you could have from one or two to as many as ten or more points.

This will provide you with a somewhat ordered list of what you could say in this presentation. But let's not forget you only have a certain amount of time to say all this. How will you fit it all in if you only have an hour? You will have to be diligent and make decisions about what makes the cut and what doesn't.

- Can you cover a couple of points with one idea?
- Is it possible to solve some of the puzzle before the presentation or after it?
- What can be taken out without ruining your case?

Now is the time to start cutting. You will be doing a lot of cutting as you move on through the process of refining and rehearsing, so you may as well start now.

- If this is the spine of your play, then what scenes can be deleted?
- What parts can be cut?
- Do we need all of that dialogue or can we do it with a picture or analogy or some action that gets the same point across?

This is your first chance to really take control of your presentation and do it your way. Think about your audience and think about your competitors. Are there whole sections you can cover quickly, by simply saying something like, 'I'm sure our competitors will have covered the issues affecting your market (or whatever the point is that you're skimming over). Rather than using your time to go over ground you know well, we thought we'd move on to the issues that are of more interest to you right now. We've done the work of course, and we'll give you a copy of our thoughts on the issues affecting your market as a takeaway'.

In other words, you have done the work, but you don't want to bore them with it. Therefore, now is your chance to edit your play down to a reasonable size. (Or to give you a movie version of the same thought: what footage can we leave on the cutting room floor?) Having done that you're now left with what you should say.

One last point on 'the what'—remember that you don't want to start a presentation with any unresolved outstanding negatives. Otherwise they will be listening to your clever ideas through their 'yeah, but' filter. As we said in chapter 3, if you know you have a problem either kill it before the pitch or kill it as the opening point of the pitch. Clear the air. Kill it early. Now that you know, roughly, what you should say in your presentation, your next task is to work out how to say it.

THE HOW

If writing a book teaches you anything, it teaches you that words are great but they have their limits. A great deal of this book might be more compellingly presented with pictures, or sounds, or play acting, or with song, or with the many, many variations in tone that a great speaker might use to communicate an important point.

The same point applies to your presentation. You can write the whole thing out, and it might make a very persuasive case, but in all likelihood it's going to be boring. And remember a reader can put a book down and start again at another time. You can't do that for a presentation. Your audience/judges are stuck there watching (and believe us, waiting) so you're going to need some light and shade—some colour and movement, some laughs maybe, a death scene perhaps, definitely some drama, and very definitely one brilliant memorable moment that summarises all you've said and done (the hook).

What you need to answer is this simple question: 'What is the most compelling way to communicate this point?' But first some provisos—if each of the headings on your list has a number of points under it, we aren't suggesting that you work out a different way of presenting each of those points. That would end up looking and sounding like a stand-up comic in the middle of a circus during a bombing raid. Just a little too much.

What we're after here is the natural ebb and flow of a truly great play. There will be quiet moments and there will be powerful ones as well. There will be points made by a spoken word and others that might be made by the entrance of a star, or the beginning of a video or the introduction of a piece of technology that they've never seen before.

But the task of the Pitch Leader remains: how to compellingly make this point? Consider the presentation as a whole. It is possible to do the whole thing on PowerPoint (we'll cover the pluses of PowerPoint and all the other options in the next chapter). But let's face it, a whole presentation of PowerPoint slides is like a silent movie with a bad voice-over. Certainly, you can begin the process of working out how best to say it by putting down each headline and supporting point as a PowerPoint slide. But that should simply be your starting point.

From there you will probably have dozens and dozens of slides (we've seen presentations with hundreds), from which you've got to begin building some interest. This allows you to begin to shuffle the order of the slides and key points so that on paper you're starting to get a logical flow to your narrative.

Next, see what slides can be simplified. What slides can be changed from words to a picture? What points can be made, not with slides at all, but with a pause, or a direct one-on-one discussion? Are there sections that can be taken out entirely and replaced by something really graphic—for example, if you were making an analogy of Company A's current IT systems, you might use as a prop the oldest existing computer you could find. Or you might use an abacus and make the same point.

All we really ask you to do is *think* about what you're doing, and consider how interesting it is to see and to hear. Consider what points you can make that might be dramatic and contentious. Can you challenge their preconceived notions in such a way as to jolt them into wakefulness? Can you frighten them with a possible future that they might live in without your business to partner them?

In our experience there is very little consideration given to the sheer drama that a great presentation can contain. Your aim is to have these potential clients leaving your presence inspired and motivated, electrified by your thinking and galvanised into action—the first action being to give you their contract. But none of that can happen unless the Pitch Leader closely studies each of the headings in their 'should say' list, and thinks carefully about how best to say it. This lies at the heart of everything and is vital to your success. So that's *how* you say it.

THE WHEN

Most plays have acts and scenes. They also have intermissions. Bad ones have people walking out. Great ones have people stamping their feet asking for more. But they all have a flow. The flow of your play needs to be carefully worked out. Now that you have 'the what' and 'the how', you should have a better idea of the kind of pacing required to get across your key answers, and the best place to put the hook.

Some things are straightforward enough (although rules are made to be broken and if you feel that it's right, feel free to break them). You know that you need to include introductions to your team. Introductions are tricky, and we talk about the best way of handling them in the next chapter—but we'd assume that they take place at the start of proceedings.

The final act (forgetting about the farewells and sincere handshakes) will normally be the part where you literally ask for the contract. Questions can be asked by your judges all the way through, or just at the end. That's your decision, although no matter what decision you make, the panel will very often ask questions when they feel like it, no matter where you place the Q & A point on the agenda.

So you have introductions, the end and the Q & A. Which leaves a fair few holes to fill. The first and fundamental question is: 'When is it best to tell them your answer?' That's why they're sitting there. It may be a great joy for them to meet your wonderful staff, and we bet the coffee is just great at your place, but in the end, they want to know the answer. They are desperate to be delighted with your solution. Trust us, they are desperate. And it's your job not to disappoint.

But first you need to know something very important, and that is: 'What is the Key Decision Maker (the most senior person on their side at the pitch) likely to want, and how fast do they want it?' Most businesses we've seen use a very logical flow. This is well and good, but many of the entrepreneurs who run companies these days have very little time and want the answer as fast as they can get it. They don't really have time to waste while you move with glacier-like inevitability to the brilliant conclusion you've drawn.

They don't want the slow build of irrefutable facts, supported by evidence, anecdote and witty one-liners; all they want is the answer so they can be someplace else.

Therefore, you have to know this. We've never pitched to Sir Richard Branson (although we'd love to), but it doesn't take a genius to work out that he isn't going to hang around for an hour or so as you build you case. He wants to know 'Why you?' with as much potency and power as you can muster, and he wants to know it in about ten minutes.

That kind of individual is everywhere these days. Therefore, this is one of the reasons why you've done so much work before the presentation, regarding the personalities in the business you're talking to. If the top banana is a quick-fire decision maker, you better know it. It makes the flow of the presentation much easier if you do. Because then you know that the presentation can be focused first on the answer you have, and the rest of the presentation is simply explaining why it's the right answer.

As a case in point, when we presented to Bob Mansfield when he was running Optus (the first competitor to enter the—until then—government monopoly of telecommunications in Australia), we knew Bob to be a guy who didn't like wasting time. So we told him the answer, which was the 'yes' advertising campaign, and then spent about thirty minutes explaining why it was right and bringing it to life with examples of how it worked at every level. He loved it and he bought it right there and then.

But then of course there are decision makers who are far more studied and deliberate in their actions. You need to know this as well, and consequently build your presentation piece by piece, fact by fact until you reach the only possible answer. Which of course is the one that you have. So the flow of your performance, and the answer to the 'When?' comes from your understanding of your audience.

You will be given clear signals as well by your understanding of who will be there on their judging panel. The more people there are, the more likely that each of them wants a box or two crossed off their personal 'how does this affect me' list, which you would have learnt in your interviews with them.

You will also get a hint from the amount of time you've been given. The more time you have, the more likely they want you to do a thorough job. Of course that doesn't mean that the point about when to give them the answer isn't still valid. In fact, if you can solve their problem in half of the given time you'll probably be loved by one and all. Therefore, once you have an understanding of your audience and the time you're given you can make a decision about where the highpoints of your presentation are going to occur and can place each item in the right place at the right time. The final part of the play is the casting.

THE WHO

We talked about the casting of your presentation, since it's one of the first issues you have to consider. Now comes the bigger decision, and it's a tough one. The people you've assembled have done their jobs and hopefully have helped produce a masterful piece of work. Sadly, they probably won't all have a role in the play when the curtain finally goes up.

When you see great drama at the theatre, you don't see the writer and the director on stage as well as the actors, or a cluttering of lighting technicians and props people. That would be ridiculous, of course. Yet unfortunately this thinking often invades presentations, and you will see people who don't say a word sitting quietly watching. Meanwhile, the prospect is thinking, 'What is that person doing here?'

This is the tough part of being the Pitch Leader, and this is what we called earlier the 'push in the back'. A lot of people have worked very hard to get you to where you are but, sadly for them, they won't be on stage. There are many reasons why not—time, personality fit, experience and competency are just a few. But there's no point in being nice about it. The people who you cast have got to be brilliant in the role you give them. Their performance reflects back on your whole business. While we're big fans of stumbling sincerity, we'd prefer just sincerity, without any stumbles. So you've got to do the hard job, work through what you have to say and decide who is best to say it.

In the course of the pre-pitch there may be one or two people who have taken a primary role in dealing with your prospect.

Therefore, Company A will expect them to be there, and they should be unless there's a very good reason why they can't attend. If they can't be, or they've been given a push in the back, it's wise to explain their absence at the beginning, when you're doing introductions. You never know, someone on the judging panel may have fallen in like with them and will be missing them now.

Deciding who best to do each task in your presentation is quite straightforward—simply consider who best fits this particular job. We've explained the value of proper casting, so won't belabour the point, but whoever takes a seat at the presentation is there to do a job, and to do it brilliantly. Our simple rule is: 'The only reason someone is in the pitch is because if they weren't there we might lose'.

The idea that anyone should be rewarded for all their good work by having a seat in the pitch is plain wrong. Here's an analogy that explains it.

Kicking a Goal for Victory

Say the Australian Wallabies are playing the New Zealand All Blacks in a Bledisloe Cup rugby final. It's been a nailbiter right down to the wire, but with thirty seconds to go, a big lumbering Wallaby second rower has scored in the corner, and the Wallabies are just a conversion away from winning the cup once more. (Sorry if you're a Kiwi.) That forward has done a sensational job to get the Wallabies into a position where they can actually win the game.

So now the Wallabies captain goes over to our hero as he's gasping for air and he says, 'Mate, that was bloody magnificent. Now I want you to kick the conversion to win it for us. You got the try, you deserve to have the kick for goal'. Can you imagine that happening? Of course not, the team would mutiny!

No, naturally the captain will give it to his best kicker, because he knows the best kicker gives him the best chance of winning the game. No matter that the bulky second rower did all the work to give them the chance of victory. Now they need to use their best resources to finish the job. Yet how often have you seen or been in a position where somebody is given the chance to kick a goal in a presentation, and the reason is 'They've worked so hard, they deserve it'.

Bugger that! You want to win. If that means that the guy who's worked fourteen days without sleep to get you the answer you're all looking for is told, 'Sorry, but you won't be in the presentation', well that's the way it's got to be. There is absolutely no room for sentimentality. It *is* hard, which is why having shorthand expressions like a 'push in the back' helps, because it takes some of the personal issues out of the equation. You'll win more often too.

TIMING IS EVERYTHING

Now that the four key questions have been answered—the what, how, when and who—the Pitch Leader has to determine the amount of time each of the headings will require. Let's not get ahead of ourselves—we'll be dealing in detail with rehearsals, and cutting the guff and editing what isn't necessary in the next chapter, but at this point you still need a loose idea of how much time each section will require.

The longer each section takes, the more important the 'how' becomes. One person droning on for twenty minutes, repeating endless PowerPoint presentation notes, is a pretty good definition of eternity for the average viewer. Therefore, think about what needs to be said, and also consider who is going to say it. Remember that humans are funny. People who seem diffident and shy can suddenly believe that they have a natural gift for banter and repartee once they're on their feet.

Unfortunately, you don't want them to discover this on the day of the presentation, but alas, this sometimes does happen. We've seen people who were terrified before the big day stand up and slowly grow in confidence to such a point that the allocated time they had is blown clear out of the water.

On one memorable occasion in a pitch we were involved in, a guy became so enthralled by his own genius that he would not shut up, and we had to, quite literally, push him away from the overhead projector.

(Can you imagine the sheer tedium of a guy who thinks he's not only right, but witty and right? It was hell, and we didn't win the business—although amazingly he complained to our bosses for the way we interrupted him.)

It was actually the best thing about his presentation. It was over. So when you're working out how to carve up the precious time you've been given, err on the side of less time, not more time. People will more often than not talk more, not less. So give them less time to start with and go from there.

We've also found that being very precise is a better way of making people think about the time they have and the things they must say in that time. For instance, it's better to give someone eight minutes rather than ten minutes. It underlines the importance of precision and it gives relevance to the idea that, 'The presentation went like clockwork'.

REVIEWING YOUR HANDIWORK—ENTER THE DOCTOR

You should have a clear idea of the way your presentation looks and sounds now. You should have a clear running sheet and your agenda can be written out on your whiteboard in the war room.

At this point the Pitch Doctor needs to be involved so that they can cast a critical eye over the flow, the key points and the people involved. It's their role to ask the tough questions of the Pitch Leader. They need to see this exactly as a critic would review the synopsis of a play.

- Does it have a story?
- Are the points being made in an interesting way?
- Does it build to a conclusion or set up a premise for the next presenter?
- Is there enough time for the main answer to be clearly explained?
- Are the right people in place?
- Does it make sense?
- Does each point flow logically from its predecessors, or are we telling them 'why the butler did it' before we've told them 'the butler did it'?

All those close to the presentation lose that objectivity. The Pitch Doctor knows the story you need to tell and ensures it flows sensibly.

You can see from these fundamental questions the key role that the Pitch Doctor plays, and the importance of their relationship with the Pitch Leader. Trust is everything. If either thinks the other is wrong, they must be able to say so. But equally, the Pitch Doctor has to understand that in the end it's not their decision. The Pitch Doctor provides feedback initially to the Pitch Leader alone. They can debate things heatedly if necessary, but in private. Once the Pitch Doctor is convinced that the Pitch Leader understands their point of view, they must, like all others, accept that it's up to the Pitch Leader to make the final call.

It's very important that the Pitch Doctor has the courage to say what they feel, the knowledge of the subject and the individuals involved so that they can give a point of view with confidence, but they must also have an ego that doesn't need to dominate.

In other words, they don't want to be Pitch Leader.

breathe

the hook

'A man must get a thing before he can forget it.'
Oliver Wendell Holmes

FINDING THE HOOK

We hope that this book is full of useful information. But nothing in this book is more important than 'The Hook'. The hook is what makes something memorable, or clever or remarkable. There are hooks everywhere—in art it's Mona Lisa's smile; it's Van Gogh's thick paint and incredible colours; it's Goya's way with observation; it's the way that Monet could see light and paint light better than any other; it's the sheer majesty of Michelangelo's Sistine Chapel, or the look on the face of Mary in his *Pieta*, or the perfection of his David. In music it's what gives you goosebumps when you hear Beethoven's *Ninth Symphony*; it's what made the Beatles so great, their music was full of hooks; Sinatra's hook was his phrasing; Elvis' was his sound and his movement. In movies the hook is any one of a number of scenes in *Casablanca*; it's Clark Gable as Rhett at the bottom of the stairs in *Gone With the Wind*; it's Clarence the angel in Jimmy Stewart's *It's a Wonderful Life*. Hooks are wonderful, marvellous, miraculous things because they lift our spirits and make a moment remembered for a lifetime.

It's called a hook precisely because of that—it hooks into your brain and won't let go. If you think about the music you love there's bound to be a great hook in it, something that connects the sound or the words in a special way directly to you and how it makes you feel. It strikes a chord and resonates with you. If you consider art and the things you love about it, there will be pieces of art that touch you in special ways. The hook is in all of that somewhere.

So what place does the hook have in a business presentation? You aren't making music, you aren't trying to make art, so what relevance does the hook have for you?

The hook is everything. Because the hook should be the one thing that sticks in their heads long after you're gone—the one thing that they remember about your presentation, above and beyond everything else. So later, when they review the presentations they've seen, they'll be able to say, 'Wasn't it great when they did that?'

What you're aiming for is a hook so good they will remember it forever. Not just the theatre of it, but *the point of it*. This applies to every kind of business and every kind of pitch. Even a simple presentation made by one person to two or three others needs to have a hook. But naturally the hook will change in its scope.

It's wrong to think that a hook is purely theatrical, that it must be tricky or full of starbursts and fireworks. A hook can be very quiet, very personal.

So as you consider what the hook is going to be for your presentation, don't discount the small but brilliant gesture; it can be truly memorable if handled properly. The only thing you must remember is that the hook has to be relevant. It must be absolutely integrated into your answer and must spring directly from that answer. This point is so important we'll say it again—the hook must spring directly from your answer. To give you a clearer idea of what we're talking about, we'll give you some examples of hooks that we've seen, heard about or created ourselves.

GREAT HOOKS
The Living Example

Every advertising person knows the story of the Allen, Brady and Marsh pitch to British Rail back in the 1980s. For those of you not in advertising, here's how it went down ...

British Rail put out the brief to half a dozen agencies and waited to see what they should do. It's lost in the mists of time whether Allen, Brady and Marsh were first, second, third or wherever on the pitch roster. What is known about that remarkable day is this.

British Rail had decided to go and see each of the agencies, so they arrived at A, B and M's at the appointed hour of 10 am. As they approached the receptionist she was on the phone and seemed to be carrying on a private conversation; she motioned for them to wait. They did so with reluctance. When she'd finished her call a few moments later she asked in an off-hand way what they were there for.

With rising irritation the top guy told her that they were from British Rail and they were there for a presentation. This didn't seem to register very highly on her radar screen, but she motioned for them to take some rather battered looking seats next to some dog-eared magazines in a rather dimly-lit and dilapidated corner of the foyer. With some dismay the judging panel sat down to muffled concerns of 'unprofessional', and 'disgraceful behaviour' and the like.

After more minutes of fruitless waiting the receptionist, with a remarkable degree of indifference, asked them whether they'd like a cup of tea. They said they would. When it arrived, pale, lukewarm and in several cracked or chipped cups, things were looking pretty bad for A, B and M and their presentation. Finally, after waiting for twenty minutes in this rather dreary, dismal place they'd had enough. As one they stood up and headed for the lifts; the top guy went to the receptionist to tell her that they were leaving. It was at this point that the Pitch Leader from A, B and M appeared and said, 'What you have just experienced is an example of the kind of service your customers receive every day from the staff at British Rail. You don't just need an advertising idea, you need a business solution that you can deliver and then promise in a great advertising concept. Now, would you like us to show you how you can achieve that?'

Brilliant. And what courage! Naturally they won the pitch and that story has gone down in folklore. What a hook! Allen, Brady and Marsh will show British Rail exactly how British Rail treat their customers, and then give them a way out of the hole they've created. How could they fail? With such remarkable honesty, how could the judges not believe every word they heard for the next two hours? Now that's a hook! But there are many, many others. In each case just ask yourself: 'What idea or point are they landing with this hook?'

The Autograph

We had a pitch to a very prestigious client where everything seemed equal between our competitors and ourselves. But during the process we discovered that just about everyone on the client's side believed that one person on our side could make all the difference in the world to their business. The guy they had their eyes on was a very, very senior person in our business and was one of the true stars of the business world.

Our presentation was polished and professional and went for a little less than an hour in the mahogany boardroom of this big and powerful enterprise. At this point our guy, who also happened to be Pitch Leader, played the card. He talked about his time in the business, the successes he'd achieved for other businesses and all the mountains he'd climbed along the way. He went on to say that if we were successful in this pitch he realised that he would have to make a number of very significant personal commitments to this business, and they were commitments he wasn't sure he could make. He said that if he were to take on this role, he'd have to be prepared to make a number of promises, and in fact would probably have to sign a binding agreement to the effect that those promises be kept.

Then he took out of his jacket pocket a letter, addressed to the CEO of the business we were pitching to. Our guy said, 'I'd have to be prepared to make those promises and sign this letter'. He slowly read the letter to underline the key points. He said, 'That kind of commitment is difficult to give to you. And I spent all last night thinking about whether I should sign it or not, even whether I'd even mention it at all. But it occurred to me that yours is one challenge I've never had to face in my career, and I'd like to do it if I can. So I'm going to sign this letter of commitment to you'. And with that he signed the letter.

The relief in the room was palpable. 'Thank God! He's signed, we've got him!' It was as though this client was pitching for our business! Naturally enough we won the day, and our Pitch Leader kept all the commitments he made. You have to have balls to do something like that.

You Kill Them

We had a situation develop with one of our largest clients who had decided that he'd had enough. His was a very large business with a nationwide network that also required servicing. It was a $40 million contract.

A relationship problem emerged between our interstate office that ran the account and the marketing director, and he had decided he wanted to fire us and appoint a new agency. We'd had a lot of trouble with this particular client and we were informed that they were not including us in their pitch.

Alex Hamill had just taken on the CEO role at George Patterson Advertising with national responsibility and his first contact with this national client on his first day in the new role was to receive a fax telling him that our interstate office was fired and we had lost the national account. He'd planned to meet them for the first time that week.

It was clear that the marketing director was immovable in his decision to exclude us, so Alex rang the company's CEO. He got a call back from the CEO's secretary to say that the CEO was aware of the nature of the enquiry, that a decision had been made, and the CEO had nothing to add and would not be taking his calls. Alex asked for an appointment the next day only to be firmly refused.

So he got on a plane, flew to the interstate capital and arrived at the CEO's office. He introduced himself to the secretary who was befuddled how he could possibly be confused that he had a meeting with the CEO. Alex replied that he was very clear that he'd been refused, but he was here anyway. A quick call to the CEO resulted in the same response, 'He won't see you'. So Alex said, 'I understand but it's not acceptable. I intend to wait here in this office until I get a meeting with the CEO'. An embarrassing situation, but once they realised he was serious the CEO relented and invited him in. Alex explained his predicament of being day one on the job and put the case for including us in the pitch. We're in the persuasion business and Alex is a great persuader. The CEO relented and invited us to pitch.

You can imagine that if we had a bad relationship with the marketing director before this, it was now openly hostile; his decision had been overridden. But we've got a philosophy that 'as long as the client's got a pulse, we're a chance'. We were dead before, now we were alive and that's progress.

Then we swung the Patts machine into action. A whole new campaign, new creative teams, new account teams, new value adds. But a marketing director who hated us.

We followed our disciplines of extensive research and even though the competing agencies had signed confidentiality agreements and were

{ the competition }

Don't be afraid to find a way to undermine the possible answer that the other guys may have given. Do it as subtly as you can of course. Innuendo is all that might be needed. Or a well-placed leak to the press.

Whatever it takes to win short of larceny is fine. After all, most of the time no one on the judging panel really has much of a clue what the really, really right answer is anyway. So all you are doing is helping them love your solution, and you can help that process along by getting them to fall out of love with your competitor's answer.

sworn to secrecy about the pitch and their involvement, we found out who we were up against. The thing that amazed us was that the agencies the marketing director had chosen to pitch were all small- to medium-sized companies, many with no national network to service the local needs of dealers/agents and interstate offices around the country. So we kept this to ourselves. This was potent information, but it's important to know how and when to use that type of information to full effect.

We developed a great campaign, rehearsed the presentation and went into the pitch. We presented well but the body language was obvious. For the marketing director we were just going through the motions. And it was clearly going to be his decision. However, we think that the CEO quietly admired our tenacity.

Then we brought on the hook. We knew that the CEO (and probably the marketing director) had no concept of what it took in terms of manpower to service the account. We thought this was the single most significant differentiator between us and the opposition and had developed the most effective way to slam home this point with the hook. We said, 'We know that you've chosen agencies A, B, and C to compete for this account'. The look on the marketing director's face as it turned red with rage was priceless. The CEO said, 'I thought that was confidential'. The marketing director agreed that it was. Clearly embarrassed, he demanded to know how we knew. We responded, 'Well, you didn't tell us so I guess that just leaves them. In a highly competitive industry like yours where you need to share confidential information with your agency, I guess you'd have to ask the question "If they can't shut up about something as simple as this, what can you trust them with?" But that's not the main point. The main point is that Agency A only has thirty staff in one city. Agency B has sixty staff in two cities and Agency C has forty staff in one city. We have five hundred staff across the country. Do you realise what it takes to service your account? Let us demonstrate'. We walked to the door and opened it. In filed *every* person who worked on this account from *every* city in Australia. They began to line the wall of the room and as each reached their designated spot they introduced themselves by name and in one sentence explained the role they played for the client. It took over twenty minutes for the sixty people to go through this process.

We then showed the organisation chart and how they interfaced with all the divisions of the company's head office and their dealer/agent network and their interstate offices. 'So', we said, 'we're confused as to why you could possibly jeopardise your business by firing all these good people who collectively are not only more experienced on your business than any of our competitors, but actually outnumber the size of each of their entire companies?' The CEO looked at the marketing director and said, 'So am I'.

The marketing director stumbled for an answer and said, 'They'll be able to gear up for it, and hire as many as they need'. To which we replied, 'Yes, but that will take months. And with every week worth over $10 million in sales, why would you risk a stumble for even a day? Surely you can see that we have a great creative solution, we've made significant changes to improve the key people on the account and shown extraordinary added value in our fee structure *and* we acknowledge that we must have screwed up to get into this predicament. Why don't we all chalk it up to experience? You've given us the kick in the butt we needed and you've got better advertising and a better deal'. The marketing director was squirming but the CEO was nodding. And as he looked around the room we could see that the second reason for this expensive hook started to hit home. These were not names on a chart; they were real live human beings that he was going to be responsible for shooting. We kept the account, but we were definitely off the marketing director's Christmas card list. But it didn't matter. By Christmas he was gone, and we were still there.

The Star

In September 2000 Sydney was about to host the Olympic Games. We were their agency and we'd all put in an enormous effort on the campaigns. We were exhausted, but getting ready to party. Then suddenly we were given the opportunity to pitch for the Warner Bros Movie World account. We only had a week to prepare and we were to present to the senior management of the Australian operation, and the co-owners Village, represented by Chairman John Kirby and MD Graham Burke and Warner Bros President and one of the power broker legends of Hollywood, Sandy Reisenbach.

To tell the truth, we were under-prepared the day before the pitch. The ideas were pedestrian and when we reviewed what the team had done we didn't want to present any of it. So we got some fresh thinking on the team and went back to the drawing board. That night as we went to the opening ceremony of the Olympics, we were concerned that we would disappoint with our presentation the next day and be embarrassed in front of people for whom we had the greatest respect and who had provided us with the opportunity because they trusted us.

Our rebrief to the team had been: 'Warner Bros. Movie World advertising has forgotten their reason for being. It's become like every other theme park promoting new rides and experiences. This place is different because it's "where movies are made". It *is* Hollywood on the Gold Coast but their advertising isn't showing that. Give us some Hollywood magic. Our advertising has to have as much magic as the movies'.

The next day we saw a script that delivered that. A concept which saw a kid enter the park with her family and her face light up as she saw the magic and wonderment unfold before her. Then a super hero flew into scene, scooped her up and flew her off hand in hand like Peter Pan and Wendy, to giggles and amazement. As they flew around the park we saw all it had to offer, finally delivering her back to her delighted family now all sitting in a carriage in the daily parade. Lots of fairy dust and lots of family warmth. It was a good script but not a great idea. We needed a hook, and we found one.

When we presented the thinking, the clients were nodding in agreement. When we presented the script, they liked it a lot. But probably not enough to change agencies. Then we said, 'Last night at the Sydney Olympics opening ceremony, the standout that captured everyone's hearts was the little girl who unpacked her things alone in the middle of the arena and then flew up into the sky. That little girl's name is Nikki Webster and she is going to be a star one day. But more importantly she's going to be the star of your new commercial. We cut the deal this morning and she is signed exclusively to us, for you'. The clients couldn't believe it. They were gobsmacked that this little girl who'd hijacked the opening ceremony was going to star in their commercial. We won the business then and there.

The Commitment

We were in a pitch against a number of agencies, including the incumbent. The client had created a very famous catchphrase about ten years earlier, but had walked away from it about four years ago. We really believed that this catchphrase was the solution to their problem, in that it was a powerful branding device which they desperately needed and we thought they'd wrongly dispensed with it.

It's unusual for an ad agency to tell a client that they don't need a new idea, but rather they need to go back to an old idea that someone else had created. We had nothing new to excite them with, so the thing we needed to impress on them was how committed we were that this was right. (Maybe they could walk away thinking 'They couldn't come up with a new idea so in desperation or for expediency they've told us to go back to an old one'.)

We went through all the thinking, the research and we even talked them through a couple of scripts we'd written. It was a successful presentation without being a bell ringer. At the very end, after they'd asked their polite questions and been given straightforward answers they got up to leave.

At this point we said, 'You know we told you that we believe in that catchphrase of yours. We really think it can work for you. In fact, we believe in it so much we've actually produced, at our own speculative expense, the scripts we just showed you. That's how much we believe they're right for you'.

We'd *never* done this in a pitch before. You often prepare storyboards or rough cuts using existing footage stolen from other ads or movies to help explain an idea. But in this case we'd spent six figures making the finished ads and if the client didn't buy them they'd be binned. We played them the ads, they could see we believed in what we were saying enough to risk it all to make the ads—and best of all they loved them.

We won the business with a line written by another agency ten years earlier. That's showbiz. Our conviction displayed in the investment was the hook. And women still 'can't get by without their mum'.

The Play

Sometimes it's important to actually bring the problem you're solving into sharp relief. We were doing a pitch for the Roads and Traffic Authority of New South Wales. The problem was all about bicyclists and motorists not getting on. The issue that was very clear in the brief was that there were two very distinct sides to the issue, both of which had perfectly valid points of view. But the RTA wanted one side to give way, in this case the motorists to understand the bicyclists' point of view.

We needed to bring the issue to a head in a dramatic way. The scripts we'd written showed a series of disputes between representatives of both sides. But in script form they were lacklustre. We knew they'd be great finished commercials, but in script form they were devoid of the emotion and passion that road rage evokes. So we literally brought the scripts to life. We got two people, representing a driver and a bike rider, to walk into the room, and act out the conflict. The anger was palpable, even frightening, and the passion believable.

The RTA could see that both sides felt passionately that they were in the right. Once we'd established that, we said, 'What if the cyclists and drivers actually stopped arguing and started agreeing with the other side? How would that look?' Now those same battling couples came back in one after the other. But now the bike rider began talking in a far more conciliatory way, and the driver began to see their point of view.

By stage-managing a kind of conflict resolution we'd illustrated the issue that needed to be resolved. It was dramatic and it was simple, and together with a straightforward line, 'The Road is there to Share', it won the day—precisely because it understood the issue so completely and gave an answer that was hard to forget. The hook was bringing into sharp relief emotions so raw in real life that they could never be conveyed in a script.

The Drama

There are occasions when you want to shock a prospect out of their lethargy. In this case the business we were pitching didn't even realise we were pitching them! We'd been talking to them, seeking an opportunity to pitch their account, but they were committed to the company that they'd had some success with over the previous eight years.

We managed to get into a conversation with their MD and marketing director, regarding a small retail problem they had in a small state in Australia. To them it was a tiny matter not even worth raising with their existing agency. To us it was a door wide open to display our capabilities. We said, 'Give us 72 hours and we'll give you a solution'. Since they had nothing to lose, and we'd guaranteed complete security they said fine.

What they didn't know was that we had no intention of simply solving their retail problem. We were going to solve all their problems with one giant idea. For three days, fourteen of us worked for an average of sixty hours each. At the end of it we asked the two clients to come to a discreet location where they would see our solution.

We explained that in order to solve their retail problem we first had to solve their brand problem. The reason they weren't selling was not because of poor retail offers, but poor brand perception. People didn't think much of their brand. For the next hour we rolled out the research and strategy and then the creative idea, which was to use Roy and HG as presenters for their campaign. (Roy and HG are a well-known Australian comedy act who'd never done a commercial before.) Then we showed how it worked at a retail and individual outlet advertising level.

We also knew that they were under a lot of pressure from their dealer network and dealer buy-in was paramount. In fact, the dealer network was hostile towards the company and through our research we knew that this was what kept them awake at night.

Then we took them upstairs to a studio where we had the room dressed as a dealer launch event complete with their products on the stage and an audience of dealers, made up of agency personnel. We sat them in the audience and out came Roy and HG in dinner suits and introduced the new products and the new campaign just as they would at a real live dealer launch. They were brilliant, funny and intelligent and had the audience enthralled as they pitched our campaign to the prospective client and their dealer network.

The whole campaign came to life and they could see it unfold by looking at it through the eyes of their dealers. They knew that their dealer network would love it and love them. Three days later, $25 million worth of advertising account changed hands and the incumbent didn't have a clue that they were in any danger. In fact, three days prior the client was very happy with their agency.

WHERE DOES IT GO?

The final question to answer is where do you land the hook? For that you need to go through your agenda and work out where the hook would be most effective. (By the way, the hook isn't an agenda item, it's woven into the presentation seamlessly.) Therefore, the best way to set the hook is simply to work out where the answer is revealed and place the hook there.

It's also possible that the hook is revealed slowly as your case develops. That might be in a situation where you are in a unique venue, such as a pub, and slowly but surely the reason you are there begins to dawn on your audience. Or you can punctuate your presentation with a dramatic revelation of the hook, at a decisive moment. You just have to think about where is the most effective place to land it, and that requires careful consideration of both your answer and your audience.

WHAT THE HOOK ISN'T

Just to make absolutely certain we've explained the hook and its role completely, we'll now tell you what the hook isn't.

The hook isn't going to unnecessary effort for no purpose. For example, years ago we saw a presentation to a major supermarket chain by one of our interstate offices. The agency had spent a lot of time and trouble creating an entire fruit and vegetable stand that they placed in the presentation venue. This would have been fine if their idea was all about freshness, or if the fruit and vegetables were important to what they were going to say, or were props they used in the presentation. Sadly, the vegetable stall seemed to be there simply to show how much effort had been put into making it. It was theatrical, but not relevant to the main point.

The trouble was, for the people they were talking to, a vegetable stall was actually kind of boring, since they had about three hundred of them all around Australia, and all of them looked better than the one in the presentation. That's an attempt at a hook that isn't a hook.

Similarly, there have been attempts to use a venue as a hook. Venues can be terrific for setting the tone of a presentation, but they have to very clearly link back to the answer you're proposing. Using an art gallery as a venue is fine if your point is about creativity or expression or originality (or any number of other things come to that). But if it's simply to have the presentation in a different location to the normal, then that isn't a hook. It may provide a purpose but it's not a hook.

What it comes down to is simple: every presentation needs a hook, but the hook must spring straight from your answer and underline the answer in your judges' eyes. Anything else is a gimmick and a complete waste of time.

WE DON'T ALWAYS GET IT RIGHT

Once we were preparing for a presentation in our boardroom and some workmen had been doing repairs to a sideboard in the room. It was unfinished and unsightly so we just threw a black drape over it to hide it from view. Unfortunately the client thought that the big idea was under there and would be dramatically revealed at the appropriate time. So he didn't pay much attention to our ideas because he was waiting for the big one at the end. When we finished he didn't believe we actually were and said, 'Come on, stop teasing us, show us what's under the cover'. Oh dear.

breathe

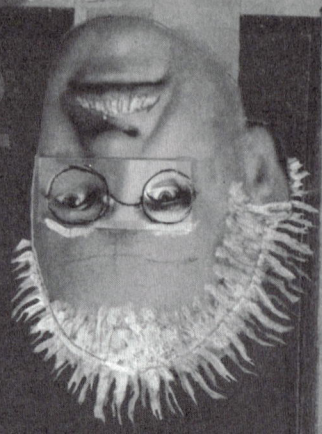

{ step 5. stagger }

fiddly details

'You need three things in the theatre, the play, the actors and the audience. And each must give something.'
Kenneth Haigh

In this section we'll go over everything you will need to know to make your presentation the best and most memorable case for Company A giving you their business. We'll look at all the fiddly details that you might not have considered before. We'll also be covering points that will happen on the pitch day itself, but that need to be prepared earlier. That's why we're doing it now.

It doesn't matter whether you're an investment bank, a telco, an internet provider, an ad agency or any other business. When it gets down to the business of winning business it's all very much the same thing. The subject may change, the type of people will change from industry to industry, but what you are attempting to do remains the same. You are putting on a show to illustrate that you have the best answer to their problem. It will be entertaining, tightly rehearsed and completely professional. It will be memorable and involving. It will leave them wanting more—of you. Ideally it will make them want to start up a partnership with you right there and then.

At the very least they're going to know that there isn't a more professional, well-versed, knowledgeable, intelligent, interesting and thoughtful bunch of individuals in your industry than you and your team. So we're going to put on a show. And it's going to be fun. Now let's start at the beginning.

YOUR PLACE OR THEIRS?

This is the first and most fundamental decision. Sometimes you have a say in this and sometimes you don't. In pitching for large contracts they like to have the presentations at their place, because it's simply easier for them. Other times the prospect wants to actually see the type of people they will be dealing with by visiting all of the competing companies on the pitch roster. They want to get a feeling for the vibe within the business. They want to see how professional each competitor is and how well they manage the tension of the pitch. So very often there isn't any choice. Company A will say, 'It's happening at our place on Monday, 15 December at 10 am'. That's it. Or they might say that they will be seeing you at your place at a nominated time and date.

First question then: 'If you have a choice, what's better?' Nearly always the answer is your place, simply because of the obvious reasons. You feel more comfortable there and you can control it much better. It is generally true to say that the home ground advantage is one that you want to have if you can get it. But there are exceptions, which we'll get to.

Second question: 'Do we have any say in the time and the place?' Don't be afraid to ask for what you want. As we've said earlier, there is generally a Gatekeeper at their end who decides these things. Just how they're decided can be a bit of a mystery, so don't hold back from asking for what you want.

You must think of a very good reason why you want to move the presentation from their place to yours, or from one time to another and generally if it's too close to the date the chances are things won't be changed. But that's why you've already got some kind of relationship with the Gatekeeper—you know enough about what's important to them and their company to have used any possible reason to move the presentation to where you want it to be. They can only say 'no', can't they?

IF IT'S THEIR PLACE

There is no feeling quite like walking into a room you've never been in before to begin a very important presentation. It's terrifying. And in some ways it's meant to be terrifying. This will sort the wheat from the chaff.

A new environment can put off the most experienced player. To use a horse racing analogy, even the champions of the turf will be taken to the racecourse prior to race day to get acclimatised to the new surroundings. Horse trainers know that horses perform better in a familiar environment, which is why they allow their horses to 'have a look'.

Therefore, we strongly recommend that you allow your own team of thoroughbreds to get acclimatised to the new situation. Just as for the racehorse, unfamiliar surroundings can put people off, cause anxiety and add another level of uncertainty to what is already a difficult time for everyone. There are a number of things we suggest you do, to take away that uncertainty and to make for a more comfortable and more successful presentation.

Having a Look

If you are told that the presentation is being held at the client's place here is what you must try to do: find out if it's available for viewing.

The trick is to ask early enough. If you wait too long it will be more difficult to get in there. The Gatekeeper may have objections and depending upon how strongly they are held you can push around them or clarify your position. Often the objections they have will be simple ones—they don't want to give you an unfair advantage or they believe that it would be inappropriate, that kind of thing. Of course there will be industries where security is a vital issue so you need to be sensitive.

However, if you explain that you only want to be in the presentation room for five minutes, that you are quite happy for them to be present the whole time and that your only reason for asking is to ensure the best possible presentation to the judges, it's quite possible they will agree.

Once you've determined whether you're allowed to take a look, next you ask how many people can be taken along, to get a feel for the room. Again, security will be an issue in some cases, but if you've done your job and got the Gatekeeper onside it shouldn't be too difficult to get all of you along to have a look. If the answer is still 'No, you can't', then ask if it's possible to have someone take pictures of the room. If that's not possible we'll tell you what to do in the next section.

Ask if it's Possible to Photograph

Once you've got yourself into the room, whether by yourself or with as many of your team as possible, ask the Gatekeeper if it's possible to take some photos. Don't ask this before you get there, though. It's more than likely they will say no. But if you have your camera with you, then you are simply doing them the courtesy of asking permission.

Explain that the reason for the photographs is so that you can work out the best possible set-up for your presentation. Also tell them that the team members who couldn't be there will feel more comfortable seeing the kind of room they'll be working in.

Once you have agreement to photographing the room, do a very thorough job of it. Every issue needs to be answered, just as if you were 'casing the joint'. You will get a feel for the room and will answer many of the following points while you're in there, but taking photographs of everything will jog your memory and may give you more ideas for surprises and the theatre we'll be talking about soon.

Take pictures of the equipment that's in the room that you could use for the presentation, front and back. Make sure the machines are all working perfectly of course before you take these pictures. This is just a safety precaution in case you need to reset things like TVs or VCRs or are using their PowerPoint hardware. The reason we suggest you do this is that you never know how sneaky your competitors can be.

We had an occasion where we were following another agency into a presentation and one of the people we'd got close to during the course of the pitch called us over and said, 'You better take a look behind the TV set, I saw (famous name goes here) fiddling with the set after their presentation'. Sure enough, he'd unplugged the AV and re-plugged it so that it wouldn't work. Full marks for trying, although that is pretty dirty. Luckily we had someone who was on our side among the judging panel and we also knew how to correctly re-plug the hardware. We won the pitch too.

Take someone who is expert at IT or presentation tools such as AV equipment. This point can't be emphasised enough. You're in an alien environment using tools you have never used before. It pays to take someone along who knows all the ins and outs of projectors, PowerPoint equipment, videos and the rest. Very often the Gatekeeper will be equally clueless as to how to use the equipment, and chances are there will only be one person in their organisation who can actually work the room. It sounds silly, but it is the truth isn't it? How many people in your business can operate your various devices flawlessly? So the key is to get your expert talking with their expert to get comfortable with what's available.

Take Measurements of the Room

How long is that wall? How deep is the window? How much room is there between the table and the wall? How many chairs can fit at the table? You may think this is being excessively precise, but if you're getting a poster enlarged to make your big point come to life, you want to make certain that there's a wall big enough to hold it. This way you can guarantee you know the answer. It also underscores the professionalism of your team and the precise nature of all the various elements coming together. You have left nothing to chance.

Check where the Power Sockets are in the Room

The reason for this is you might decide that the AV system will be powered from a particular power source that you choose, rather than the one that they always use.

Find out What is Moveable and What Isn't

Can the tables be moved and if so, how quickly? Some boardrooms have very impressive, very heavy tables that can't be moved without a crane. Other rooms use tables that would be embarrassed to be seen in a canteen. Either way, you want to know what you can do with the room layout, and how fast you can do it. All this knowledge will help you plan your show to maximise your individual stamp upon the event.

Look for Any Opportunities within the Room

Don't forget that what you're after is something that you can use to make this room into your own special theatre. You will be putting your mark upon this presentation and anything you can discover within the room that will help make your presentation unique you want to find.

It may be that the room has powered curtains that you can leave drawn, but open to theatrically reveal some part of your pitch. There may be a door that opens into the presentation room—very often if it's a boardroom that door will be the kitchen—can you use that space for any spectacular effect or surprise entry?

Just as importantly, how long does it take for the lights to go down if you want to show some video? There's nothing more pregnant than that pause between the lights going down and something about to happen (you hope). If the length of time is more than fifteen seconds, you need to know that, rather than find out on the day and make with lame wisecracks to fill in the time. That is death.

Check for the Best Light Source

Some rooms are like tombs with no natural light. In that case you need to consider whether you can use the lights in the room to best effect. How do they work? Can you use them to spotlight something on a wall to heighten the drama? We just want you to think about every aspect of this pitch and leave no shot in the locker.

Also consider the time of day you'll be pitching. Where is the sun? Does it get into the room? Are the blinds needed? Remember that if you are sitting with the window behind you your audience might not be able to see your faces. On the other hand, reverse roles and you can't see their faces. You have to think about this, which means …

Think about the Seating Plan

You want to consider where you think it's best for the judges to be sitting. All in one bunch like a jury or scattered around the table? Do you want to have specific people in specific places? Think about this as you look at the room. Is it important that the CEO is closest to the screen?

If it is, where does that place you? All this needs consideration as you plan your big day.

Look for Other Rooms Nearby You Can Use for Your Own Purposes

You might like to get there early to set up or go through your charts for the last time. Maybe you just want a place to relax, if that's possible, before your starring moment. Whatever you want it for, it's nice to know you have a room available to your team. And if you don't ask you don't get, so don't be afraid to ask.

Ideally you want a room that's nearby, since it will make everything a little smoother. But don't baulk at having a room on another floor if that is what you're offered. After the offer is made, then you can ask for it to be made available the day before the pitch. Think of it like your beachhead as the invasion begins.

Ask if it would be possible to Rehearse in the Room

This is a biggie and very often will be met with a flat refusal. But again, you don't want to die wondering. Also, if you phrase it carefully, you might just be able to use that as your method of getting a particular spot on the pitch roster, first up in the morning for example. That way you would rehearse the night before and have everything set up and ready for the next day's performance.

Rehearsing in the room is a huge advantage, so even if you don't get a chance to do so near the presentation date, if you're given a date even a week earlier—no matter that you probably won't have your material ready—grab the chance anyway. It'll give your team a wonderful opportunity to get to know the environment, and you want to grab any advantage you've got. If they won't let you rehearse beforehand ...

Ask if it's possible to Get There Earlier and Set Up the Room Your Way

If you don't get a chance to rehearse in the room, the next best thing is to have some time to get prepared and set up the room as you want it, not as you found it. Whether this is allowed depends on how long you need and how much time the judges have.

Some presentations are spaced on a day-after-day schedule, while others are on a conveyor belt in-and-out. Therefore, the answer you get is likely to depend on their schedule. If they say no, it still might be possible to get more time for set up, by asking for the slot first up in the morning, or the one after lunch. Anything you can do to get an advantage, grab it.

What if They Say No to Everything?

Yep, that happens. Some clients won't give anybody the slightest advantage; they want you on their terms. These people are also generally the most difficult audience, with little feedback and very little interaction. But it's also possible that businesses putting large contracts out to tender want no hint of impropriety, so won't allow any advantages to anyone.

This means that you have your people, all your props, all your ideas and tricks assembled into one large pile that needs to be wheeled into the presentation room, set down (without revealing any of the answer) and all of this happening while your judges look on with bemusement. There might be one or two who say something helpful, but most often they seem to enjoy the discomfort you and your team are undoubtedly feeling.

So what do you do? In a phrase: take charge! Have you been to a concert where the act on stage gets everyone to clap, or wave their hands? Most people do, right? Have you been to a speech or a seminar where a speaker will ask the audience to do something, like stand up or turn to the person next to them? Most people will do it. Reluctantly perhaps, but they will follow the leader. The same psychology needs to be applied here.

When you walk into a cold room, and are expected to perform right there and then, it's the equivalent of the Christians and the lions. And you know the way that turned out. So somebody has to stand up and make a case for a little preparation time. The Pitch Leader needs to take control of the room, they need to speak with either the Gatekeeper (if the Gatekeeper happens to be in the presentation), the person running the show, or to the group of judges as a whole. And they need to say something like this: 'We want to give you our best possible presentation. To do that we need a few minutes to set things up as we want them. We know you have time pressures, so please take the time we use setting up the room out of our allocated time. We'd ask that you leave us for about five minutes, maybe you can check your calls or grab a coffee or a comfort break, but we really appreciate your understanding'.

In no case we've ever heard of or experienced has the prospect not agreed. Even if there are some dyed-in-the-wool prats on the judging panel, they will be outweighed by more reasonable souls. The group psychology takes over.

IF IT'S YOUR PLACE

All the issues that you worried about because the pitch wasn't on your own turf you don't need to worry about. What a relief. Now you have to worry about foreigners on your soil. How will you greet them? How will you make them comfortable? You have to think about the feelings that you would have had if the positions were reversed. The difference of course is that the judges don't have to put on a show for you, indeed they don't even need to look interested. But that doesn't mean you shouldn't think about the best way to handle their arrival and departure.

Remember that we're still not talking about all the things that will happen once the presentation begins, we're only concerned about getting your judges into your venue with as much care and consideration as possible. Here are some things you need to consider and answer appropriately based on the type of people and company you're presenting to.

How will They Arrive?

You need to find out how your judges are going to be arriving. Very rarely do they all arrive together so you need to establish this several days before the big day and then recheck on the day prior to the presentation. The best thing to do is simply ring the Gatekeeper and find out from them. You want to know as clearly as possible (without being an irritation) precisely how each judge will be arriving.

If they come by taxi or on foot they will make their own way to your reception area. If they are arriving by car, you can either offer to valet-park for them or organise for them to park in your car park and have someone waiting there to escort them to reception.

Who will Greet Them?

Any security tags should naturally be ready and waiting at reception, and the receptionist should be briefed very thoroughly on the pronunciation of names. This small but important point underlines the care that needs to be taken every step of the way. One thoughtless action or inappropriate word or mispronunciation can kill anyone's enthusiasm for your work.

There's no need to go for fawning sycophancy (not unless they actually like sycophancy), but you must remember the niceties. Just as the best restaurants and hotels make people feel welcomed, so too should your business do what it can to smoothly offer the best possible experience.

How are They Taken to the Presentation Venue?

Once they've been welcomed at reception, or in your car park, they need to be shown to the right location. Just as in the best restaurants and hotels where you are shown to your table or to your room, so to with a presentation at your place, you must follow the same procedures.

People can get lost, they will feel out of place and also it gives your team a chance to interact with them with some pleasantries. However, the art of small talk (which is what this is) is a gift that some have and some don't. The host needs to know how to handle both the talkative judge and the sullen, withdrawn one. Once the host has taken their guests to the presentation room they can introduce them to the Pitch Leader.

Who Shows Them the Little Courtesies?

When the host brings the guests up from the reception area they can make a point of showing them where the bathrooms are. This is a small but considerate thing to do. You might also consider having a room near your presentation room that they can use if they wish to make any calls. You will more than likely be having a short break (unless the presentation is less that ninety minutes), so having the convenience of a room they can use in private is a nice, thoughtful gesture.

How will They Leave?

Once your presentation is over you don't want the judges to slowly file out while your team do high fives and talk about how well the whole thing went. Much better to have the Pitch Leader escort them down to the street or to their cars. Once again, it's simply good manners. Besides, you might get some valuable feedback or find there's an opportunity to continue the conversation at another time.

If there are more than six or seven of them, and you need to take two lifts, then have someone who had a senior role in the pitch be the other escort. You can also organise for taxis to be ready and waiting if you have enough warning.

All of this illustrates the benefits of planning and foresight. None of it is especially startling, but frankly very few companies ever think of these small gestures that help their prospects feel more comfortable.

WHAT ABOUT ANOTHER VENUE?

We've spoken of the two usual presentation locations, their place or yours. But of course there is a third possibility, and that's to do your presentation at a different venue entirely. Whether you do this depends upon two things: will they let you and is it relevant?

The first question will be answered by your understanding of the kind of business they are and the kind of people you think them to be. You need to be sure that they will be comfortable about this. Your homework should give you a sense of what is right. You might think that the only chance you'd have to move to another venue is when they agree to have the presentation at your place, but that's not strictly true. It is possible to move a group of judges from their location to another one, if you're sure that they will be happy to do this. It's a call that needs to be made by the Pitch Leader and, if possible, floated past one or two of the people you've gotten to know over the course of the preceding couple of weeks.

If you've got a feeling that they will be intrigued by this move, then do it. How you do it is straightforward enough: you have to ensure that the total elapsed time doesn't go over the amount they've given you. So they have to be back in their room within whatever timeframe you've agreed on.

You need to get them there as easily as possible, by walking there or by car or even mini-bus. The mechanics of this means that the Pitch Leader will walk into the room where the judges are and say that there's been a change of plans and your team is waiting at another location. If there are murmurs of disapproval say that it's because what you have to show them and talk about is best done in this location. So you can see it takes a bit of courage. On the other hand it also adds another level of excitement that they won't find with anyone else.

But the big question is: 'Why?' The answer is that the new location must have a fundamental purpose to the overall presentation and is part of the hook. You could move to an international hotel if in that hotel there was something that couldn't possibly be displayed and presented at their place or yours. Cars for example, or some kind of theatre that wouldn't be possible anywhere else.

You might want to use a venue that has a particular view (see the following story).

You might want a venue that delivers a particular idea, such as an art gallery. You might do your presentation in a venue like a pub, if you were talking about meeting the people.

As you can see there might be a hundred different reasons to use a venue other than their place or yours. But it will always come back to the simple question, why? And the answer to that has to be fundamental to your solution of their brief.

Moving the Client

We were pitching for Sydney Star City Casino. They had a temporary casino and were doing very well, but they were building a brand new place over the road. Their offices were small and dismal, rented in the city. We didn't want to pitch to them there. We also knew that one of the key issues they had to deal with was moving their customers from the old venue to the new.

For that reason we arrived ready for the presentation, walked into the room and asked the six of them to come with us because we had something exciting to show them, which we couldn't do from where they were sitting. We had two limousines waiting (casinos are relaxed about the use of limos so wouldn't be outraged at this kind of showmanship) and we took them on a short drive to another venue. This was a room we'd booked at a hotel overlooking the old casino and the new one that was being built.

In the room we had all our team, with all of the presentation ready to go, with all the glitz and glamour required to make our key points. But of course the key reason we changed venue was because we wanted to show them—really show them—the key issue that they needed to solve: getting the punters from the old location to the new one without losing any along the way.

Similarly, we wanted to make sure they understood that the task they had to solve was the baggage that the old building had with it; a little downmarket, not the glamorous casino that people would imagine. It was only when they could actually see the two buildings that we could really land our hook, and we did it so successfully that we won the business the next day.

That's a good example of when it's right and relevant to move to a new location other than their place or yours.

breathe

the fun begins

'Nothing is so simple that it cannot
be misunderstood.'
Freeman Teague Jr.

Now you've got everything together you can start your final preparations. By now you will have done all your homework and know the individuals at Company A and their particular issues. You will have come up with a brilliant answer that solves their stated problem in the brief as well as the unstated problem(s). Your agenda would have been worked out to cover all the issues that will help you win the business and minimise any issues that might get in the way.

You will have pre-tested your answer, if possible, with people you trust on the judging panel. You will have decided on the starting line-up for the presentation from your side and determined exactly how long each person has to make their case. You will know the venue and the time and made plans accordingly. The hook has been worked out and you've found the right place for it in the presentation. So now you're ready for the fun to begin.

DRESSING THE ROOM

The room is your theatre and you need to think of it that way. Whether at your place, theirs or some other venue, you need to find a way to own it and make it exciting—and if possible in some discreet and clever way have it reflect the nature of your answer.

Things are slightly different and more difficult if the presentation is being held at their place, so let's discuss setting that up first. What you are aiming to do is create an environment where your idea and your people stand out from every other competing business. If you simply walk in and sit down and start talking you may run the risk of blending in with every other company that's gone before you and will go on after you.

You want to create a space that is your own unique theatre. That's why you've gone to the trouble of finding out where all the electrical points are and what tricks the room may have to offer. It's also why you've had the chutzpah to ask the judges to leave the room for a few minutes. In that short space of time you can create a whole new room—and the effect can be startling for the judges.

Walking back into a room that has been rearranged will jolt them out of their lethargy. It will also heighten the anticipation of what you have to say. It also stamps you with some authority. It slightly shifts the balance of power. It says, nicely, that you're in control.

If you have charts and reveals, you will have placed them in the best possible position—the position that you have chosen, not the one that you may have been given. You also may have rearranged the seating. You will have used place cards, with the name and title of all of your team, as well as the name and title of everyone on their side. (Neatly handwritten cards are perfect, especially if there are people who you haven't met on the judging panel. You can find out their names from the Gatekeeper—and their correct spelling and title – and quickly do place cards for them when they are out of the room).

These place cards are a simple trick and work wonders. Make sure you use large type and print double-sided so everyone can read it from anywhere in the room.

People will nearly always sit where they're placed, and there's no longer any confusion about remembering names and titles. For the judges it's simple to look at the place cards of your team and understand the role of each individual in the presentation. You can also use place mats and have your team's photos, their titles and the agenda all set out on the mat so that the judges can make notes and know exactly who everyone is. By making these physical changes to the room you've placed your own distinctive stamp on proceedings. Now it's your room. You are in control.

How you then dress it depends upon your answer and how much time you've got. Simple is best, but make sure that whatever idea you have runs through the room dressing fluidly. What you're after is a feeling of expectation as the judges walk in. They want to be interested in all that you've done and be placed in the perfect seating position to see it, and to have clear eye contact with the individuals who will be working closest with them. If the venue is at your place, or somewhere else that you control, you obviously have a lot more time and control over what you do.

The feeling you're after is exactly the feeling that theatre-goers experience before the curtain goes up. The room should be dressed in such a way that gives them a sense that something exciting is about to begin. You might consider using music as a background, before your presentation begins. Something appropriate to the occasion and to your answer. It fills the awkward silence and sets the scene.

The room dressing is once again a matter of taste and it clearly needs to spring from the answer you have, without revealing that answer of course. Having things under wraps is always a good way of increasing intrigue and it makes the whole room feel more exciting to be in. Something great is about to happen; that's the feeling you want as you walk in the room.

EQUIPMENT AND PROPS (TIPS AND NO-NOS)

Technology is changing rapidly and who knows what will be coming down the pipe as you read this. But these days a PowerPoint Presentation (PPP) is an almost automatic choice. We see them everyday and depending upon the level of skill of the people or the business that's presenting they can vary from very good to 'Oh my God, is that the time?'

There is no longer any magic in them, they have merely replaced overhead projectors (remember them?) as the presentation tool of choice. They have become so commonplace that something needs to be done to break the mould. That something is your own creativity.

A PPP can cover a multitude of meanings. It can be used for a presentation that has bare words on slides, which is fine if you haven't got too many slides and your presentation is very short and sweet. Just as easily, it can be an entire bells-and-whistles presentation with DVDs and props built in so that the whole thing is like a Hollywood movie. So one thing is clear: the quality of the PPP depends on the quality of the creator.

How competent are you at creating a brilliant PPP? It's no crime if you can't put together a great PPP, just so long as you know someone who can. In our experience it's very often a PA who has the weighty responsibility of creating the PPP, simply because PAs are supposed to do this sort of thing. There's no need for this to be the case. Who is the best person in your business at creating PPPs? There's always one and they're usually too busy.

We recommend that you either upskill your PA in PPPs or you outsource their production, with the final presentation burnt onto a single CD. It's also no issue to be technically incompetent, as long as someone in the room knows how to fix the problem. Oh, and that someone better be on your side.

Therefore, when creating a PPP your first thought is going to be: 'What needs to be said and how creative does this need to be?' To answer that you only have to look at the solution you're providing. Look at the flow of thinking that you have created in your agenda. If it's a steady build-up of evidence to the final conclusion then you need a PPP that hits like an axe. You want fewer diversions as you deliver your conclusions. Slam the points home with the power of logic and the force of persuasion. On the other hand, if your answer needs more light and shade, or indeed if you work in an industry where entertainment is expected, then a more elaborate show needs to be created.

Continue to think of it as you would a play (or movie). What things need colour? What points need explanation? Where's the climax? How do we find a happy ending? If you use your agenda as a script and you think of the PPP as a theatre or film production you will be able to more easily place the necessary highlights.

You need to think creatively.

What points can you cover with a picture rather than words on a chart? It's not difficult to come up with wonderful images that much more effectively evoke an idea than words alone. For instance, if you're talking about your experience in the Asian market you can either have slide after slide that writes out that experience line by line, or you can have pictures of Asia and its peoples as a backdrop to your words. What would you rather look at?

But don't fall for the trap of only doing this kind of thing once or twice in your PPP. You have to commit. This also means that your presenters will suddenly find themselves having to speak from the heart, rather than from the slide. Just as powerful is the juxtaposition of words and picture, if you think the words will help the understanding of the point being made. You can be creative and you can be very evocative with the right words and pictures.

We once needed to talk about the first atomic blast at Hiroshima. It was an analogous introduction to a point we wanted to make about the client's business. The best way we found to talk about that horror was to simply have on a slide the words: August 6th, 1945. On the same slide was a picture of a wristwatch worn by a man who must have been literally blasted into infinity. All that was left of him was his watch, and seared forever on its face the time he died: 8.16. You can't get more evocative than that. What it always comes back to is the answer you have and the tone you want to create.

PPPs can also be projected onto a screen or, more personally, viewed from your laptop, the decision to go one way or the other is really a function of the number of viewers you have. The more viewers there are the less likelihood there is of your choosing to go down the open laptop approach. Equally, if there are more than two of you doing the talking, it's going to look downright uncomfortable with just an open laptop for company. However, don't be afraid of using a laptop alone if it's a small presentation because it makes for an intimate pitching technique and virtually guarantees that you will have a relaxed and conversational style.

Summing up, PPPs can be beautiful things, but they require a great deal of thought—it's not good enough to just put your presentation in bullet points on a slide. You need to think about it.

And know this: passion beats PowerPoint every time! PowerPoint can get in the way of your people. Let them shine! That's the truth in a nutshell. If you're up against a team of people who pitch with passion, that passion will beat the most brilliant PPP, because passion is something you can't fake. So if you use a PPP, make sure you bring the passion with you as well. But while PPPs are the number one choice for presentations today, there's no need for it to be the automatic choice. Sometimes there are even more effective ways of making a winning pitch. For example:

Handwritten Sheets

There's a simplicity to just neatly writing a number of points onto pages of a large layout pad and using that as your presentation. For a start it says that you are no-nonsense. It also says something about you and your business—it's solid, it's honest, it goes against the trend. It can also evoke confidence or intimacy if you're well prepared. It can also convey 'last minute' or 'unprofessional' if you're not.

There's also nothing stopping you from adding cartoons to handwritten sheets to make it more fun, or you might use a pen to highlight points and circle them, or even add new points as you go. The beauty of this kind of presentation is that it's guaranteed to connect you very closely to your audience.

In a typical PPP the viewer will be turning their attention from the projection screen to the speaker, never being absolutely certain where to look. With handwritten sheets you and the layout pad are locked in together. You're closely connected to the pad and what words are on the pad and your audience. You can have the pad supported on the table and you can turn the pages as you go. You can put the layout pad on an artist's easel and do the same thing. It's also quite dramatic to tear off and discard each sheet as you go.

Just remember that you don't want the audience to read through the sheet on top to see what's coming next. Either use thick bond paper pads or use every second or third sheet and staple the two or three sheets together. Also, for ease of usage, turn up the bottom corner nearest to you so that the sheets are easier to grab and turn.

How much information do you put on the sheet? As little as possible to make the point. It's that simple.

The type of presentation you're doing will determine whether this is the right technique for you. The smaller the audience the better it is.

The simpler the solution the more likely you are to think of a simple presentation style like this. It fits with the thinking and it makes the whole pitch a great deal more relaxed. If that's what you're after, or if you simply want to stand out from the crowd, then this is one very easy way of doing it.

OVERHEAD PROJECTORS

How many overhead projectors (OHPs) are gathering dust in forgotten cupboards in businesses all over the world? Or perhaps even more likely, how many are hidden under the table for that dreaded day when all else fails? It's easy to feel sorry for the poor old OHP, and not just because they are more often on the floor these days than on the table as the centrepiece of a brilliant presentation. Maybe they have had their day, but no less a person than Edward de Bono uses one. So maybe an OHP presentation isn't such a lateral thought.

> There are only two things to remember if you're using an OHP:
> 1. If you are using acetates, build a simple cardboard frame so that the acetates slip neatly into place.
> 2. Don't fiddle with it!

If you've seen an OHP presentation you will also have seen the presenters constantly fiddling with the acetate to get the words square on the screen. Don't do that! If you have the cardboard frame you don't need to worry about it, and if you don't have the cardboard frame, put the acetate down, centre and straighten it in one go and leave it!

You can certainly use a highlight pen if you want to. Or you can do what de Bono does and have a roll of acetate and use a marker pen to make points as you go. It's extremely effective and once again, compared to PPPs it's a helluva lot more connected and interactive.

So, why not give that humble old dust-covered OHP a second life and use it in a presentation? You'll get points for being different and there may be members of the audience who will remember with fondness their own years of using the OHP when it was the tool of choice. They'll probably mark you higher for trying.

Printed Boards

These are like handwritten sheets only much more stitched-up. They can be a virtual PPP but without the need for a laptop. The boards themselves can be any size, and they have most of the advantages of the handwritten sheets—simplicity, interactivity and connection between the presenter the board and the audience—plus one giant advantage over anything else: they stand up by themselves.

This may seem a small point, but it's not. A PPP moves forever forward, and once you've passed one slide it's gone. With printed boards you can take key points out and put them around the room for emphasis and as reference points during your presentation. This means that the audience always knows what points you think are important and they have the ability to refer back to an earlier point with ease.

The limitation with boards is also their advantage. You can't have too many of them, so you are destined to have a really interesting presentation that depends on the power of your answer to carry it through.

There are two ways to work with boards. You can either have an assistant hand them to you, using the presentation table as your easel, or you can get an artist's easel and work with them like that. Remember that the audience is there to hear you, not to concentrate on your boards, so keep close to the board and use them for emphasis of each point. You also need to be aware of any eye-line issues, so check to make certain that all those people who need to see the boards can see them—that's why you set the room up the way you have.

One very simple tip that helps is to have what is printed on the front of the board reduced in size and also placed on the back. That way you don't have to get into any awkward positions to read what's on the front of the board, since it's right where you can see it. You can even just handwrite what you need to say on the board for quick reference. This very simple tip really makes things easier—it even shows you which part of the board is top and which is bottom, something that isn't straightforward if the board is unmarked on the back.

Props

While we have seen handguns and even on one memorable occasion an M15 machine gun used in a presentation, that was a long time ago and the world has changed. It's very doubtful that anybody would feel too comfortable using a weapon as a prop today. And goodness knows what the audience would think as they rushed out of the room. No, props need to be appropriate for the purpose for which they are used, and that is to highlight a point or to land an idea. They can even (obviously) be the way the hook is landed.

You don't want a presentation that's littered with props (unless you are talking to the Clean Up The World people), but you do want a presentation that will live in the memory, and the right props can help there. If your idea is something precious, maybe you can use a diamond as a metaphor. Alternatively, if you want to talk about the danger of parallel importing and counterfeiting, maybe getting a really great piece of cubic zirconia will do the trick. Whatever the prop, it is essentially a talking point—something that stops people and makes them think. It can be interactive, but if you hand it to your audience be prepared to lose their attention to what you're saying until they've finished looking at it. You may want to let them hold it and look at it as you continue talking, but don't think you'll be able to land any points because they can either read what you've given them or listen to you. Not both. Wait till they've given it back to you, then you can land the blow.

Props are a fascinating way of bringing things to a head, to underline an observation or to create interest and intrigue. But never forget what you are using them for—to underline a key issue and have it hit home with an emotional force.

Using Videos/DVDs

With the use of PPP and DVDs the humble video is becoming a bit of a dinosaur. But that doesn't mean you might not have cause to use one, or be forced to use one. Many businesses still have the video monitor hooked up to the VCR and will suggest you bring along a video to show your work rather than put it onto a DVD and play it on a computer.

So first you must know how to work the video. How bloody obvious is that? Yet how often have you seen presentations where the video presentation comes right after ten minutes of apologies, false steps, phone calls and scratched heads? Sad, but true right?

That's why you...

1. Went to the scene earlier and found out how to work it, and/or
2. Found the person responsible at their end and asked them to help beforehand, and/or
3. You brought your own tech wizard with you.

It's so much more professional to have all this ready and waiting for you. It also shows you've actually thought about it earlier rather than hoped like hell it would be okay and that things would somehow 'work out'. Under no circumstances rely on the people you are meeting to play your tape for you. After all, how competent are you at getting all your electronic gear working?

HANDLING YOUR WORK

Whether your work is a detailed proposal for a $60 million telco deal or a well-written document or a beautiful print ad—handle the work like it was precious. People have sweated blood for this. The least you can do is handle it with the reverence it deserves.

Don't just toss it onto the table—hand it over solemnly with great respect for the intelligence that created it. Chances are if you treat it with respect your prospect will too.

THE BIG TEASE

One last thing on props, handling the work and showing boards and so on—don't tease people. It's a common mistake for presenters to have something they are about to show their audience, but before they show it they pick it up and keep it with its back towards the room, so that the audience can't see it. They then talk about what they are going to reveal, when of course everyone just wants to see it.

Instead of picking it up and then not showing it, you have two much better alternatives: a) talk about it first and then pick it up and show it or b) show it and talk about it. To tease them, talking about something that you will soon let them see but not right now, is truly irritating. Because nobody really likes being teased.

breathe

{ the three-stage mission }

There's a fundamental truth about winning pitches that needs to be understood right here and now. When you are in there on the big day pitching for the contract—you're at stage two of a three-stage mission. From our experience in over hundreds of presentations in many diverse businesses, pitches are won in three stages, not one. And as a three-stage mission, the way we see it is that about 30 per cent of the points are won before the presentation ever happens. Forty per cent are won in the presentation itself and the final 30 per cent are up for grabs in the days (and weeks and months sometimes) after the presentation. Think about this for a moment from your own experience, either as someone who has been pitched to, or as a member of a pitch team.

{ step 6. walk }

almost there

'Seventy per cent of success in life is showing up'
Woody Allen

Now everything is in place. All you have to do is make sure it's perfect. And the only way you can make sure of that is to rehearse. Actually, you should rehearse, rehearse, rehearse. Broadway shows have castings, walk-throughs, rehearsals, dress rehearsals and out-of-town tryouts. They also have rewrites, recasting, re-editing, reworking, re- just about everything. They take the trouble to get it right and they plan it as a fundamental part of their production; same thing with your pitch. You need time to get the performance perfect; what follows is the way to do it.

THE FIRST WALK-THROUGH

Using your agenda as a guide, each individual knows how long they have for their part. As the Pitch Leader you have discussed with them the role they are playing. You will have explained the important points to be landed. They will have a clear idea of why they're saying what they're saying. They know what the point of the presentation is, they will know their part in the answer and they will have an idea of what the hook is. You've told them all this either as part of a group or one on one. Either way, they get it.

Now comes the time when you do the very first walk-through. This is where everyone shows their stuff to each other. That means that everyone who is in the presentation attends, no exceptions. Essentially this is walking through the pitch, like the walk-through in a play or film.

Everyone gets a sense of the content and the flow. At this point don't worry about the overall length of the presentation, just take note of the time it takes each person to say their part. It's quite likely there will be plenty of things still to come, from completed PowerPoint slides to props. But right now all you are concerned about are six core questions:

1. Are they saying the right things in the right way?
2. Does it make perfect sense?
3. Does it have a solid flow of logic to it?
4. Does each point come at the right time?
5. Are there moments of light and shade?
6. Is the right person doing the talking?

There are three people who can comment on those six questions—the Pitch Leader, the Pitch Doctor and the actual player. It's important that the rest of the team don't critique other team members. Feedback is a sensitive skill. Many people are offended by criticism from their peers. This in turn causes friction among the pitch team that can often show up in the final presentation. Clients can sense it.

Assuming that you are the Pitch Leader, be aware that it is a very raw emotional time for most people—standing up and talking, trying to put across a point of view while people are staring and implicitly looking for faults. Therefore it's natural for people to be nervous and defensive.

This is when you need to have a sound appreciation of everyone's ability. You need to be able to make the decision on whether or not the nerves they are showing now will be under control on the big day. You have to make your mind up whether they are doing the total job you're asking of them—not just speaking, but communicating, genuinely engaging the audience, being warm and connected to the audience, exuding professional competence, being part of a powerhouse team.

After they have done their first walk-through tell them how long they took to say what they said. Ask them whether they felt comfortable with what they said. Did they feel that some points could be made better? In other words, let them tell you how well they thought they went.

Remember that you're dealing with people at a very fragile moment. Now isn't the time to mention anything that they might take as a personal slight, however well intentioned. Now is the time to be pragmatic about *what* they are saying and simply be focused upon that rather than worry about the quality of *how* they're saying it.

It's generally at this first walk-through that you get the feeling whether or not the player is right for the part. Sometimes things will have changed from the time you cast the role. Maybe you discovered that this prospect appreciates a different skill set or a different age group. Or you may have found out that the prospect thinks of you as being too inexperienced to handle their business. Which might make you re-think using a 25-year-old graduate to do this part of the presentation. Whatever happens now depends on those six core questions. If you think they could be answered better by someone else, then now is the time to say so.

This is why having shorthand expressions like the 'push in the back' is so helpful. It makes the process less personal. If people are aware that there is a chance they will get the push, they know that there are many reasons why it can happen. It isn't simply because they were bad at whatever role they were asked to play. So if you decide that someone else can do the job better, simply say in this case, 'Sorry, but I'm giving you the push in the back'. This shouldn't happen at the first walk-through. It should happen afterwards when you and the Pitch Doctor have had a chance to discuss it all, and we'll go into the best way to do this in a moment.

You and the Pitch Doctor also look at how it might be possible to make every presentation a little stronger. Referring back to those six questions, you decide whether there are better ways of saying what needs to be said. You will determine whether each point could be made with more power and effect. You will decide whether the story holds the attention or wanders. You will have timed each presentation and seen where things needed to be changed, shortened, eliminated or amplified.

Using those six questions as your guide you then debrief the team, both collectively and individually. They can all have an opinion about the flow of the pitch and its impact. But they *cannot* have an opinion about any of their fellow players. That is not their role and it isn't their decision.

You take everything on board, but you and they understand that this isn't a democracy. You are the person who has to make the tough calls, with the aid of your Pitch Doctor as counsel and advisor. But as always, it's still your call.

You leave that first walk-through with an idea of what is and isn't working. Your Pitch Doctor will help you with that. Now you need to give feedback to each individual in the pitch, prior to the first rehearsal.

HONEST FEEDBACK

No one enjoys being criticised, but everyone wants to be better. So you must walk the fine line between truth-teller and supporter. That's why it's important to have some framework to use as you debrief and give feedback. Using the six core questions will help you, because most of them can't be taken personally.

The one that can be taken very personally is the push in the back. When you tell someone that they have been cut from the presentation, you must tell them honestly. In the cases where you are pushing them in the back because they are not good enough as a presenter you have to tell them this too, and offer advice and support. Then ask them to stay on and help with the preparation of the pitch. It may be that someone else does their presentation, in which case they can help enormously. It may be that the points they cover are now going to be covered in a different way. Either way, it's very important that they feel they still have a contribution to make. And of course they will still be celebrating when you win.

In our experience most people are aware of their strengths or weaknesses in the area of presentation skills, so it's most often not a surprise. Make sure they know that they haven't failed personally, which is why you still want them involved in the presentation somehow. But that doesn't make it any easier to accept implied criticism. Therefore, if they do get the push in the back, make sure that you find something about what they did that you enjoyed. It could be their depth of knowledge, or the effort they must have put in. Find something. Then tell them honestly what you felt was missing. If it's something that's based on new knowledge of the prospect, tell them that.

Tell people the news individually and give them solid reasons why you have made the decision. Then at the rehearsals that person is still there and unembarrassed when you explain that their role is being played by someone else or is being folded into some other part of the presentation. Or cut entirely.

Also, if they genuinely are not as good at presentations as you thought, get them talking about how they felt. Were they too nervous? Did they not know their stuff? Were they uncomfortable? Just engage them in conversation and discover how they really feel about it. Then offer help of one kind or another. Maybe a course, maybe an opportunity to do a presentation on a subject they choose to a friendlier audience.

If you are going to be successful then the important thing is getting the right things said at the right time to the right people. That is essentially what the push in the back is all about. It's definitely not personal.

For those who aren't getting the push in the back, the conversation is based on the other five questions. Again, talk to them about how they felt. Tell them what you thought in positive terms, and where you felt it needed emphasis or change. Little observations can make a big difference. Here it's really helpful to have notes at hand to give them specific points from specific parts of their presentation. That way you can say, 'Remember when you talked about such and such? That was when you lost me for a moment ...'

You can also take this opportunity to lighten their presentation, or suggest where they might make some cuts to their slides. After you've spoken with each of your players, they must have a very clear idea of what needs to change for the rehearsal. And through each conversation must flow a feeling of confidence and security. Remember you are the leader, their leader—they trust and believe in you. You know what it takes to win.

THE ROLE OF THE PITCH DOCTOR

The Pitch Doctor has a distinct part to play in all this. It starts with their mindset. They need to think like the prospect. That means they are watching the first walk-through, the rehearsals and the dress rehearsals with the same attitude each time: 'I'm the prospect, what am I thinking now? Do I know what they are trying to say? Am I comfortable? Do I like these people? Are they convincing me?' It's a tough role, and it's important to understand why the Pitch Doctor has to maintain a certain distance from the players.

The Pitch Doctor can't have a direct involvement in the solution, otherwise it becomes too personal for them. They have to be dispassionate. They also must have the ability to see things on a very pragmatic level, understanding that while they know that the team has put a great deal of effort in, it's irrelevant if the points aren't being landed.

They need to feel confident about what the prospect is looking for. They must also be clear in their feedback to the Pitch Leader. Point by point they must know what is working and what isn't. They must have a sense of where the drama should come. They must know all the tricks, so that if they see an opportunity to land the point with a sledgehammer blow, they can suggest it. But remember always that the Pitch Doctor can only make suggestions and observations to the Pitch Leader. And ultimately, it's the Pitch Leader's call.

WHAT TO LOOK FOR

At the run-throughs and the rehearsals there are three things for the Pitch Leader and Pitch Doctor to keep thinking about.

1. What can be cut?
2. Where can we add drama?
3. Is it captivating?

The cutting can come from what's being said. The more people talk, the less they say. The same thing applies to slides. Make the slides punchy and pithy. And edit, edit, edit. Take out the long words, take out the jargon, take out all the terms that are bullshit and don't say anything in particular. Look out for the clichés like 'at the end of the day', 'going forward', and 'the bottom line'.

Try to instil an enthusiasm for saying things in new and fascinating ways. Look for the opportunities to say something in a clever, memorable way. Think of what's being said and ask yourself whether it needs to be said just like that, or whether it can be done in some other, more imaginative way. Is there anything that can be left unsaid, or that is understood and doesn't need elaboration?

Finally, does it hold the attention like a great play? Is there an interesting cast of characters that you become intrigued by and that keep your attention? Does the whole thing move along with a flow and a pattern that is compelling to the viewer? Or are there parts where you fall asleep, or want to get up and leave the room?

the cockpit check

'Flying isn't dangerous, crashing is.'
Anonymous

Before you launch this thing and begin the rehearsals you need to do a cockpit check. You have the agenda and its contents—all the things you will cover in the meeting. Just like a pilot goes through a complete review of all the things they need to take off safely, you must do the same. It's a sure and simple way of guaranteeing that you have left nothing to chance and that you've done everything humanly possible to ensure success. Here is the list of things you need to tick to ensure you're ready for take-off.

- Have we solved the problem set out in the brief?
- Have we solved the unstated problem/s?
- Does this presentation satisfy their business needs?
- Does it satisfy the individual needs of the judges?
- Have we avoided any nasty political issues within their company?
- Have we clearly linked the end take-out of the presentation to the fundamental business/personal needs of the CEO (or the Key Decision Maker)?
- Have we shown that we have matching values?
- Do our people match the needs/emotional wants of the judges?
- Have we pressure-tested the possible answer with them so that there will be minimum surprises?
- Have we hit all the hot buttons we know they have?
- Have we got a great hook?
- Do we know all we have to about where we're pitching (if it's not our place)?
- Do we have a compelling close?
- Have we asked for the order?
- Have we considered the possible questions and do we know what the right answers are and who best to answer them?

Much of this may seem straightforward. But then you'd imagine that a pilot sitting in their seat would assume that somebody's filled up the fuel tanks and checked that there is a path already navigated to the destination. The fact that the pilot never takes those things for granted, even the most bloody obvious things, must tell you something about what it takes to do anything flawlessly. You do not have the luxury of coming back another time and doing it again, only better. Nor does a pilot.

While you don't have the enormous pressure of safeguarding four hundred or more lives, you do have the enormous pressure of being responsible for growing your business. So following these checkpoints allows you to have the confidence to proceed through to the next phase. But before you do ...

WHAT'S SAID WHERE AND WHEN?

There's a fundamental truth about winning pitches that needs to be understood right here and now. When you are in there on the big day pitching for the contract—you're at stage two of a three-stage mission. From our experience in over hundreds of presentations in many diverse businesses, pitches are won in three stages, not one. And as a three-stage mission, the way we see it is that about 30 per cent of the points are won before the presentation ever happens. Forty per cent are won in the presentation itself and the final 30 per cent are up for grabs in the days (and weeks and months sometimes) after the presentation. Think about this for a moment from your own experience, either as someone who has been pitched to, or as a member of a pitch team.

The pitch itself isn't the be-all and end-all. If you've been a judge then you will already have some preconceived idea of the company and the people doing the pitch. Even if the only idea you have is, 'This is the first time I've met these guys'. The same holds true if you've been in a pitch where the first gut-wrenching moments take place as you realise that these people are total strangers to you. And since in our experience that is the way it is for almost every pitch in which we haven't been involved, then it must be obvious that the pitch itself is only part of the story.

Similarly, once a pitch is over, it's not over. The fact that you feel an emotional high, followed by an aching hole where your stomach should be, simply signals that the tough bit, the big day, is over. But that doesn't mean that you can relax. Because now you have to go back to the judges with follow-up material. You have to keep your name in the front of their minds. Because even if your presentation wasn't the sparkling success it should have been, you can still win. If you play it right.

Therefore, even with all this work you've done to have an agenda written out, with all the points prioritised and with your cockpit check carefully completed, there are three more decisions to be made prior to rehearsal and finding the hook.

1. What gets said before the presentation?
2. What gets pitched at the presentation?
3. What's held back for after the presentation?

Your team, if you've followed our advice, will be miles in front already. There will be several, perhaps most, people on your team who have met with the judges. Therefore the judges will know you and feel comfortable with you. Since they're only human, they will have spoken among themselves and given a snappy pen-picture of those of your people whom they've met to any of the senior judges that your people haven't managed to meet. Therefore your efforts will not have been in vain. But now you need to consider what needs to be said before these judges gather.

The issue you must answer regarding what is said pre-sell is simply this: 'What must we do to make it easier on the day for them to buy our answer?' You need to look at your answer and decide if there is anything that needs some groundwork prior to the pitch itself? For example, it may be that you will be offering a solution that will require a terrific infrastructure that only your company possesses. But in the presentation itself it might be hard to prove you have that infrastructure already in place. Besides, your competitors may say the very same thing. Therefore, you need to have shown that infrastructure to a member of the judging panel before the big day. That way you will have a corroborating witness to verify what you say is true.

The reason this is important is that quite often a question such as this isn't posed in the presentation itself. It's way too complex and may take too much time to answer, even if it is fundamental to your case. So having a witness on the judges' side allows for that issue to be answered by a very believable source—their own judge. Just how you create the situation where you get that judge to see your infrastructure is an issue we hope we've addressed in other chapters, but once again it illustrates the power of doing this kind of hard work up front, and the truth about presentations being in three stages.

Another example of where it may be advisable to do some pre-sell before the presentation is if your answer has a degree of difficulty or surprise to it. Remember that most people are inclined to look for problems when given an original solution, so it makes sense to do some background work to help that solution look more sensible or plausible. Once again the best way of managing this is to address the issue with one or two of the judges before the big day. How you handle this is to take them aside (either together or individually) and give them a glimpse of what your surprising answer might be. As you judge their response, you also give them reasons as to why they might be surprised by it. But also you give them the proof they need to believe that this surprising solution is indeed a plausible, completely viable answer to their brief. This way you once again have people on the judging team who have the ability to clarify for their fellow judges any issues that might otherwise stymie your answer.

Obviously you must be careful about which of the judges you speak to because you don't want to create any difficult political issues for yourself. That's why it's vital that you consider these issues from a position of knowledge—knowledge that only you have. Once you decide what needs to be pre-sold, then you need to decide what you hold back.

The points you can win after the big day are vital. Consider the issues that you might want to hold back, for strategic reasons.

You will see from your agenda and the flow of it that there may be points that are best left for another time, to be used as verification or for support. There might be items on the agenda that are important to solidify your case, but may simply be redundant for the presentation itself. Those kinds of support proofs can be best used after the presentation. And also, naturally there will be issues raised in the presentation that you can use to keep in close contact with the client. From that thinking you know what to pre-sell and you know what to use after the presentation.

breathe

{ finding the answer }

An Idea Solves a Problem

This is the best definition of an idea that we know.
It may not be the one in the dictionary, but it's the
best way to look at what your team is doing now.
You have all the information you will ever need.

The problem is, most people don't understand
the problem, so they come up with ideas that
solve the wrong problem. Which still leaves
the problem.

Our methods guarantee that you solve the right
problem. In any presentation for any business,
whether it's for a large property tender, a large
government contract or a prestigious advertising
account, you need an idea that separates your
offering from anybody else's—an idea that fires
their imagination.

To do this you need to think—either collectively or separately. But the thinking has to have a purpose. Therefore, the one thing you need to do, above everything else, is clearly state the problem that your idea will solve. This written statement should neatly encapsulate the key issues of the brief and the unstated problems in the business.

The answer should be easy to understand. It should be explained in a sentence or two at most. If it's involving an area where few people have a deep understanding (IT is a prime example), it needs to be translated into simple-to-understand English. The reason for this is that someone is going to go with your idea to the Chairman or the CEO of the company you've tendered to, and they're going to say what they think is your answer ...

taking control of the game

> 'In war the will is directed at an animate object that reacts.'
> **Karl von Clausewitz**

Now's the time to think about the things you can do to stack the odds in your favour. What can you do that will give your business an unfair advantage? There are two things you can do.

CHANGE THE GAME

'Is that in the Rules?' If you've done everything according to our suggestions so far you are already a long, long way ahead of your competitors. They would probably have got together whoever was available, looked at whatever the brief asked them to look at and had a go at solving the problem. They might have done some research to understand the issues a little better, they may have made some calls; they may even have gone to the trouble of meeting with one or two of the judges. But our bet is they wouldn't have done much more than that. Even for large amounts of money, most companies don't have the necessary systems in place to confidently attack any given brief in a manner guaranteed to give them the best chance to win. So they lose.

One of the most common mistakes they will make is to follow the rules of engagement set out by the client, prudently adhering to each section of the brief and answering correctly, even brilliantly. But by now you know that the brief is only a loose approximation of the real truth, their real problem. You understand this real problem because you've worked hard to do so. Now comes the time to start getting paid for doing that extra work, and going a lot deeper than your competitors want or know how to.

Your answer will allow you to construct a response to the brief that is in line with the bigger picture objectives that you understand Company A to have. That will almost certainly mean you will be offering ideas and answers in the presentation that haven't even been requested in the brief.

This may seem like a big risk, why take it? Because you know that the answer you're giving is going to solve their bigger picture objectives and the personal and emotional needs of those people on the judging panel. So the trick is simply to ensure that in answering the real problem, you keep using the original brief as your guide. That way you know you will get to the destination the brief has pointed to, but you will do so via the route that you choose. And that route will let you hit all the right places that you know will get you most marks in the presentation.

Your competitors might say, 'Hang on, that's not right, they didn't ask for that in the brief'. And they'd be right, but you know what they need to solve the big picture problem, and so long as all the judges get what they're after, you shouldn't have to worry about following any stupid rules. After all, your prospective client wants their unstated problem solved and you want their business.

To ensure you get the highest marks, there are four things to do:

1. Demonstrate that You Understand the Business Imperatives that Lie behind the Brief

You do this by the way you construct the presentation itself. You will be using as issues the very things that you've discovered are the real issues of their business. Not just the things that are set out in the brief.

2. Show You've Taken the Trouble to Understand the Prospect's Macro Business Needs

You'll be offering far more than just a supplier transaction. Your thinking and presentation will prove that you can be a true partner and have a true relationship as equals in the area of the business where your companies meet. You can only do that if you've put the hard work in and truly understood the intricacies of all the relationships within their business. That has come about from the work you've done and now must be illustrated in your presentation.

3. Explore 'Value-add' Opportunities that will Elevate You above and beyond Your Competitors

Work out ways of engaging your supplier network and other customers that will supercharge your offering. For example, access to their research and their customer database. You want the CEO to think, 'I would never have thought of that', when they hear your ideas for interconnections and value-adds. If you look at the way Company A does business and you then look at their bigger picture objectives you are certain to see ways to maximise what you have to offer them.

4. You Want to End Up Being Seen in a Completely Different Paradigm to the Rest of Your Competitors

As a Klingon would say, 'They're a business, Jim, but not as we know it'. You are indeed a different species to your competitors! If it was a four-horse race, now they're seeing three horses and a gazelle (you).

REPOSITION THE COMPETITION

It's said that all is fair in love and war. And this is war. This is no time for courtly gestures and false bonhomie. You have to be implacably resolved to win at all costs, although we won't be asking you to play dishonestly or to break any laws. Because many businesses provide a similar offering it's often difficult for the client to judge the offering that is marginally better. In that scenario you're just in a beauty parade. Therefore, the only way to win consistently is to make you look beautiful and have the client convinced all the others are ugly. Do that and you've got daylight between you and the rest.

Understand that the game will be won by the side that clearly looks to have the best answer in the minds of the judges. Because the others aren't simply not quite right; they're obviously wrong for their company. If you can put doubt into the judges' minds, so that they are uncertain about your competitors' responses, then that is to your advantage. How do you do that? Here are some ways to undermine, trap, trick and generally sabotage your competitors before they even get into the room.

Anticipate Your Competitors' Response

Every business, whether it's a bank, legal firm, telco, ad agency or insurance group will have a kind of 'fingerprint'. It's the thing that identifies them and makes them what they are. No company is perfect; every company has issues that create the image that they have. Think of the businesses that you use or work with. We guess that you could define them in a sentence or two. Similarly, you could anticipate the strengths they might play to, to convince a company to award them the contract.

Your task is to do that with your competitors in the coming pitch. You will almost always know who they are. You also know the key strengths they might have. Think like them. Do as ancient China's military strategist, Sun Tzu, suggested and get into the head of your opponent. Imagine what answers you would provide if you were in their shoes.

Once you have that thinking done, you should end up with a list of perhaps five strong points that each of your competitors might use in a pitch against you. They might be bigger, smaller, faster, older—all the obvious things—but also try and get into a more granular way of thinking: what are the small but important areas that they might emphasise to beat you? What relationships do they have? What recent successes have they achieved? Get into as much detail as you can and imagine precisely where their strength lies. Now you have to get some very tiny pebbles, and without leaving any fingerprints, lob them into the centre of that well-oiled machine that is/are your competitor/s.

A Knee to the Groin

The tiny pebbles you throw are the counter-arguments and the counter-claims and sheer trouble that you create for your competitors that could create doubt or concern in the prospect's mind. These naughty tactics and counter-arguments need to be carefully thought through. You need to determine exactly when and how to throw these pebbles to create maximum damage. You can do it with the right word from the right person in the ear of the prospect's CEO. For example, 'Jim, I hear that Smith's are tendering for your business. That's surprising considering the trouble they're having bedding down the XXXX piece of business. If they can't handle the work they've got …' You can see how the well-placed word can create trouble.

You can do it with media stories. You can do it by destabilising staff. For instance, we discovered that one competitor's best weapon was a very talented woman who had impressed the client enormously. We knew she was a key to our competitors winning the business. The client had also made no secret of the fact that he really admired her talent. So, since we were always on the lookout for talented people, we interviewed her for a job. She indicated that if it was offered to her she'd accept and we'd confirm it in two weeks.

Our pitch came around and when that woman's area of expertise came up, we said that we knew that the client had a high opinion of her work and we had some good news. As a matter of fact we'd been talking to her for some time and were pleased to announce that she would be joining us if we won the account. In fact, if we won this business it would be her primary concern for the first six months of her contract. We took our competitor's ace, added it to our two pairs and came up with a pitch, winning full house.

Similarly there are times when confidentiality is a key ingredient. We once learned that a competitor was using freelance talent to develop their pitch. We waited until two days before the presentation and asked the client if they were aware of this or concerned about outsiders being given their confidential information. We suggested they check to see if the agency had signed confidentiality agreements with their freelancers, and of course they hadn't. No matter how good their answers were the client now felt they were unprofessional and untrustworthy.

Another Dirty Story

We found out that one of our competitors was using someone who had once worked for us, and when he'd left he'd signed a no-compete clause in his farewell package. So we were surprised to discover that he was working on contract for the enemy. He was a naughty boy. But we didn't blow the whistle right away.

We waited. Until the last possible moment, and then we rang the competitor to ask them to confirm a rumour we had heard. That this guy was working for our rivals and that, therefore he and they were in breach of the contract he'd signed with us. We also told the client who was horrified. He rang our competitor and discovered that they had to lie to him to cover the truth. It put them in a position from which they couldn't possibly win. Because we timed the pebble to be thrown at exactly the right time—and that is when they have no time to recover!

So now that you've decided what to say, when and where, you can move on to the drama, the intrigue, the joy and the terror of the presentation itself. Well, the rehearsals of it anyway ...

breathe

{ step 7. run }

dress rehearsals

'The play was a great success but the audience was a disaster.'
Oscar Wilde

The dress rehearsal is the time when everything must be ready; when all the tricks are in place and you can run through the thing for real. And the reason why you're having a dress rehearsal is the same reason that they do it on Broadway—to see if everything actually works as it should.

On Broadway, if there's a trapdoor and the heroine is supposed to fall through it, they make sure she can do that while wearing the hooped skirt she has on in character. You don't want to find on opening night that the trapdoor opens and the heroine falls through as planned, only for her dress to stay where it was. Similarly, you need to make sure that all your handovers work well, that the props work and that the slides are all correctly spelt. (We doubt that any PowerPoint presentation exists that doesn't have at least one spelling mistake or literal hidden somewhere within it.) Also, consider where the audience will be sitting.

Where do you all need to be arranged to most effectively work together? Do you all move to the front of the room to present? Do some of you do your presentation from your chairs? Do you move around as you talk? Standing and talking from one place may be fine, but they don't do that on Broadway very often, do they? It makes for a fairly boring night is why. So we suggest you vary it a little bit. Move around, sit up close and talk quietly at some points; have some fun if that's appropriate at other times.

NOTES OR NOT?

Actors keep a script handy until they know the part by heart. Then they spend the rest of their energy learning how to react. Reacting is the real acting. No one has to be word perfect, but most people have a preference for some form of *aide-mémoire* that helps them recall what needs to be said.

For some this starts off as their entire presentation written out. They pretty much read this until they know what each point is they're saying—then they can shorten the written form down. Other people have more confidence, and know that as long as they have a point they want to reach, they'll make that point and hit all the right notes along the way. Still others use PowerPoints as their cues and when they dry up, press the button and remember what comes next.

There is no right way to deliver the words. If it takes more notes for some people that's fine. What you don't want to see though is a dull reading—like a bad sermon. If anyone's part begins to resemble this, for goodness sake give them the push in the back. If they haven't got the necessary confidence to do the job, you will just have to get someone else. But anything that helps your players deliver the points you need to land, from short notes, to bullet points, to a great memory, is fine.

STAYING SHARP

Some people are very good at presenting, but get dried out if they have to keep on rehearsing. If you know them well enough and are sure they can do the job, then one simple way of getting them to go through their stuff without going stale is to ask them to do it in the third person.

That way what they say is '... at this point I'll be talking about the research. Then I'll go over there and pick up this board and show them the figures. I'll move in close to the top banana and underline the point so they can see it clearly ...' You can see the difference. We've used this with a number of people and it works a treat. They still get to cover what they need to say, but they don't lose the magic that they want to keep for the big day.

Timing is Everything

Make sure that everyone is timed as they do their presentation. We've found, working with many companies, that the timing helps people understand the importance of their presentation and the need to see it as part of the whole. Nearly always when we've timed the 'Run' dress rehearsal it goes over the allotted time limit. But with rehearsal comes certainty, and as it's refined people get better and better until they can land their points in the time allowed. When your agenda has each part with a time next to it, and as each person hits that mark, bang on, it perfectly illustrates how professional your team is. You're doing your presentation with precision.

THE AUDIENCE—YOUR JUDGES

The Pitch Leader will have briefed the senior staff chosen to play the part of each of the judges in the dress rehearsal. This dress rehearsal needs to be as near as possible to the real thing—so it needs to be viewed by an audience that will be similar to the audience you'll face on the big day. How you do this is to consider each of the individuals who you know will make up the judging panel or the review committee. These are the people you've done your research about. You've given them nicknames, you know what concerns them and you've made sure each one of them 'wins a prize' in this presentation.

So when you brief your judges they must know they are playing a particular role too; you need to clearly tell them what you believe the personality of the character they are playing is like, and what drives them personally and professionally. They will try to get into the head of the individual they are playing, to think like them as they view your presentation. They'll be briefed so that each of them knows the key points you think will interest them. Their task is to see if these points are well landed.

By doing this you get the clearest picture possible of what it will be really like in the pitch itself. You place the name of the judge they play in front of each of them, so your team knows who is who. They're briefed not to be too friendly, but to play the role as well as they can. If Company A's top banana is known to be a bit of a cold fish, the person who plays that role needs to be a little stand-offish too. It all helps the pitch.

If you've done your homework you will know the key points that must be landed, and you might even know how the whole presentation will be marked. In either case, create a scorecard that allows the judges to mark each aspect of the pitch. They will use this scorecard later in their debrief. It's not possible to give you an example of a scorecard, because each pitch is completely different. But the things that will appear on it will be specific points, such as the key issues that need to be ticked off, both from the brief and from the unstated problems that you've unearthed. The scorecard will also have more intangible things such as credibility, clarity, creativity and so on—whatever the Pitch Leader considers important. Each presenter can also be marked individually on any number of criteria that you choose, but be careful and destroy the cards after use.

One last item on the scorecard is this: the one-line debrief. This allows each judge to summarise in one line whether they would or would not give your pitch their vote. You know how it is, after all the pitches have happened someone wins, and when the judges are asked why the winning business won, the answer is never a fifteen-minute discussion, it's always a sentence. Something along the lines of 'They proved they understood our culture and how to get buy-in from the staff' or 'They showed they were the only ones with the infrastructure' or whatever. And that of course is key. Because that's probably the kind of thing they will say to their Key Decision Maker when they discuss your case. It might not be the first thing they say, but it will be the defining reason why they either give you the tick, or give you the flick. You want your judges to write down their one-line summation, independently, on their scorecards.

TOUGH JUSTICE

The role of your judging panel is central to the success of your pitch, since if you've chosen them well and briefed them correctly this device is the best possible way for you to give your pitch that 'out of town' tryout which can highlight the weaknesses in your play.

Your panel have to really get into their part, listen intently and make certain that when the pitch gets to their area of interest they know exactly what to look for. They should take notes, especially they should look for where there might be areas of inconsistency: a point that wasn't followed up, or a statement that isn't supported by the facts. We all know that there are times we try to squeak things through and hope nobody notices. The judges need to be alert to any claims that are made that might be hard to believe and when the time comes they have to put whoever made that claim under pressure to prove what they say is true, or possible.

While we've said that they shouldn't be too friendly, they shouldn't be so taken with their roles that they don't have any warmth at all. They should try to look and act non-committal, in fact very much like a real judge or jury should look. Just like everyone on the pitch team, they will have the name and title of the person they are representing printed on a place card and they will be seated according to the seating plan you have already worked out. This means that all your pitch team will be familiar with the names and the seating positions of everyone they will pitch to.

'I'M GLAD YOU ASKED ME THAT'

Unless you've decided that Company A are likely to interject or interrupt with their questions, leave the questions to the end.

Here's where the judges come into their own. Each needs to have at least three questions ready to ask at the conclusion of this rehearsal. Two questions they ask should be directed at the person who they believe was responsible for dealing with the section of the pitch that was relevant to their interests. The third question should be the most difficult and challenging that they can think of. Perhaps there has been some inconsistency, or someone's tried to fudge something.

Questions are the Achilles heel of many great pitches. You must be prepared for them by anticipating what the key issues might be. The judges will also find inconsistencies and problem areas that you may not have foreseen. If the judges have asked questions that have stumped the presenters, make sure that everyone knows that this is the purpose of this dress rehearsal: to discover things you only see when you're doing it for real.

Now is your chance to work out answers. It's vital to have a thorough list of the likely questions and work out short sharp answers. We go into this part a little deeper in chapter 9, 'Fly', but the time spent working out good answers to tough questions will often be rewarded on pitch day.

THE JUDGES' VERDICT

After the Run dress rehearsal, one of the really key conversations takes place, between the judges and the Pitch Leader. This is what happens:

The presenters leave the room and are joined by the Pitch Leader. The judges remain and discuss what they've seen while it's still fresh in their minds. The Pitch Doctor will be there, listening, but definitely not contributing. They talk about what worked, whether the key points were landed, how the hook was landed, in fact everything that made up the pitch. They form an opinion. They will have their scorecards and will have filled these in independently.

Then the Pitch Leader plays the role of the Key Decision Maker at Company A. This means that the judges stay in character and debrief the

Key Decision Maker in exactly the same way your real judges will when they review your pitch. This allows the Pitch Leader to ask tough questions and to get hard answers. Because you are trying to make this exactly like the real debrief, there is no point in holding back. If something isn't working, now is the time to say it. The Pitch Doctor offers any possible ideas that might help, now that they've heard the judges' verdict.

Honesty and integrity makes for a stronger debrief. You must know the truth. Get their one-line debriefs. Hear whether there is a common thread, whether they all agree on the key point that was either landed or missed entirely. Would they give you their vote, and if not why not? Now is the last chance for the Pitch Leader to make the tough decisions—people are pushed in the back, things are cut, points are rearranged. It's now or never. But now at least you know the truth, as far as the judges saw it.

breathe

{ step 8. jump }

you pitch and you're judged

'I don't do verdicts. But I try to present all the facts.'
Diane Sawyer

This is nearly always the toughest time. Now you'll be asking them to do it again, to jump through hoops for you. You've done the dress rehearsal. It's been as close as it can be to the real thing. You will have timed everyone, you will have seen the mistakes that were made (thank God it's just a dress rehearsal!) and now is your chance to hone what you've done to a razor sharpness.

You've been debriefed by the judges, they've given you their verdict and told you what does and doesn't work.

It's all come out. They've spoken of the overall impact of what they saw. They've told the Pitch Leader in their role as the Key Decision Maker what issues were handled well and the things that still might cause trouble.

Occasionally nothing needs to be changed and everything is glory and light. Wonderful. Do it again tomorrow just like that. But more often things don't work and points aren't landed. Someone will say, 'I didn't think my issues were addressed very well'. Someone else might say, 'The pitch team didn't seem to understand what my hot buttons are'. Decisions need to be made. And it's the Pitch Leader who has to make them.

- How can we improve a particular section?
- Who needs extra presentation coaching?
- Does anyone need the push in the back?
- Can timings be tightened?

- Did the judges want to see more of certain sections? Can it be done?
- What will be lost to make up the extra time?

TELLING THE TEAM

Now that the Pitch Leader has had feedback it's time to tell the pitch team what the judges thought of it all. Be honest, but be thoughtful. Most people know when they've stuffed up and are eager to make amends.

That's the great strength of following this plan—you actually have time to fix the things that often go wrong through lack of planning. This feedback should happen as soon as possible after the dress rehearsal, after the judges have left the pitch room. The pitch team needs to reassemble immediately in the pitch room and be ready for changes while it is all still warm.

The beauty of this process also means that people understand that this effort is all about doing the best possible job. That egos don't matter so much as results. It also creates a great team bond that translates into a great vibe in the pitch itself.

Once the Pitch Leader has made the changes required—whether big or small—it's time to do it all again in front of the judges one last time. Depending upon your schedule, you can do this the same day or the next—it doesn't matter, just as long as it's done. Even if the changes are very minor, don't try to go straight from the dress rehearsal to the pitch itself. Rehearse it again. You can only improve your chances of winning can't you?

This is when it gets tough. People want to stop, to go home and not worry any more about this damn thing. Keep their spirits up. If you've a mind to, you can bring in some drinks to loosen things up a little. Maybe even tell them that you'll be taking them to dinner afterwards. Since you've blocked out this time in their diaries they haven't got anything else planned. It's called a bonding session when sporting teams do this—just don't let things get out of hand.

MEMORIES ARE MADE OF THIS

One of the nicest things you can do about now is make a record of your pitch team for posterity. Take pictures of each of them. When you win you can create a nice memento of the occasion, framed with all the participants, the date and so on. In fact when you win you might like to have something special created: a fine piece of crystal with the players etched into the glass or a beautiful treasure from Tiffanys (they do make inexpensive treasures we hear). But we're getting ahead of ourselves ...

breathe

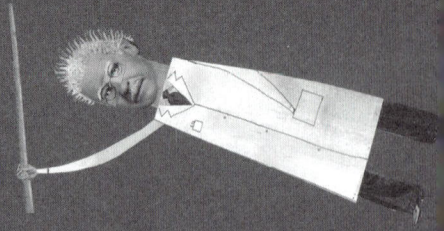

{ step 9. fly }

in the room

'... On with the show, this is it.'
The Bugs Bunny Show

'No more nursing or rehearsing of parts, we know every part by heart.' Well, that's unlikely—in fact, if you do know your part by heart you'll need to be a bloody good actor to pull it off.

You've assembled at the presentation venue. If it's your place you're lucky, if it's at the prospect's place then you need to do this somewhere nearby. Either you've arranged to be given a room in which to wait, or if they haven't allowed you to do that and you've organised a hotel room somewhere nearby, you'll do the next part of your preparation there. And then move camp at the appropriate time.

FLY THROUGH IT

With everyone in the room you simply fly through your presentation. You do it in the third person and you don't need to use your boards, PowerPoints or props. Just refer to them and that will confirm that you've got them. All you're doing is giving it one last chance to place what each of you is saying in context. The way it goes is a bit like this ...

The Pitch Leader will say, 'We walk into the room and we sit down. I will do the introductions. After that I'm going to run through the agenda and ask them if they would like to ask questions during the presentation or save them 'til then end. I'll check to make sure that we have the agreed amount of time with them and if any of them have any timing problems.

Then we'll begin. I'll show them the agenda point by point and explain your role more clearly and why you are the right person to answer that point. This will take me ninety seconds. Then I hand over to Bill who does his thing'.

At which point Bill does the same thing in the third person and so it goes through the whole presentation. You can do this in about ten minutes or less. It's simply one more way of embedding your flow into everyone's head. It further emphasises the team feeling that you want to make a highlight if you possibly can. Remember, 'People buy people'. The other essential thing that should happen on the big day is you should make the decision to win.

DECIDING TO WIN?

We've told you in chapter 2, 'Mumble', about how John Bertrand decided to win the America's Cup. Now it's your turn. The idea that you must decide to win may sound a little strange. After all, the alternative is you decide to lose, correct? Well, in truth that isn't the opposite of deciding to win. The opposite of deciding to win is not having a collective commitment to win. 'Do I want to win? Um, I haven't decided yet.' Making the conscious choice that this presentation will win the pitch is crucial to your attitude and body language as Pitch Leader.

You must exude the confidence of someone who has already seen the answer and knows it is in your favour. It means that you are channelling all the positive energy into really focusing on success. This is simply good psychological thinking. You are aiming to get into the zone, where no other outcome but victory is possible. The greatest athletes all have this attitude—they expect to win, so they very often do.

Your mental processes change once you've decided that you will win. And with that change comes real physical and mental change as well. You look more confident, more like a winner—and people love a winner. Your thinking looks for the positives in the situation. You are aggressive rather than defensive and you have no fear. Because you know that losing is unthinkable.

So you have decided that you will win. You've followed all of the advice we've given you so far (we hope) and now you're sitting down with the people who hold your business life in their hands. You want what they have. And what they have is the power to say 'yes'. You're feeling nervous; you may even have visited the toilets with a fluttery tummy—all good signals that you've peaked at the right time. You can't perform unless you have an edge to your nerves. Sir Laurence Olivier was afflicted with stage fright for a large part of the 1960s and he was the greatest actor of all time. If it happened to him it's okay if it happens to you. Just accept it.

If you haven't slept the night before, that's also pretty normal. Your adrenalin will kick in anyway and you won't feel a thing till it's over. Because you've taken the right steps, nine steps in fact, you will have a deep feeling of confidence—you know you're sitting in front of a well-drilled machine that has been tuned to perfection. You know that you have the answer that these people are so desperately looking for, and you know that the way the answer will be delivered will knock their socks off. All that needs to happen now is to unleash it. You take a deep breath, lock eyes with the key person on their side and begin.

YOU'RE NOT ALONE

You're in the room now. As the presentation takes off things will happen, mostly good to great, but occasionally bad. One of the key things to remember is that these people you're pitching to have never seen this before, so it's all fresh and fascinating to them. It should also appear fresh and fascinating to you. Which means that when someone on your side is talking, your team should be listening with the kind of rapt attention you hope the rest of your audience is showing.

You should be enjoying each other's company. You should be relaxed and having fun when that's appropriate. The only member of your team who shouldn't be looking at the person talking is the Scribe. They are in the room to take careful (but very subtle) note of everything that happens that affects your audience. The Scribe needs to have a well-tuned ability to read body language. They need the ability to judge what is being said when one judge whispers in the ear of another, just as you finished talking about the costs. Did that whispered exchange mean anything? Are we way too high? Are we surprisingly low? Is there an issue that may need to be addressed later? All these things the Scribe is looking out for. The way someone might nod appreciatively at a certain point; the awkward silence that might occur when a question is answered poorly. All of this information is silent, none of it is direct, but it all must be written down and analysed later. Because later as you go over the presentation piece by piece and work out what to follow up with, you will want to know any unspoken issues that need to be addressed.

JUMP IN WHEN NEEDED

As you listen to each of your people do their very best to convince your audience that you and only you have the perfect answer for their business, your antenna needs to be up and tuned in. If you see any missteps on behalf of your team; if there is a mistake made or an important point either missed or incorrectly presented, don't be afraid to step in and correct it. The trick is to do so without stopping the flow of the person talking and to do it in such as way as to let them retain their dignity and keep their confidence on a high. It just needs a light touch. And it doesn't have to be you who jumps in (we're assuming you're the Pitch Leader), anyone on your team can do it as long as they understand it needs to be done in the right way at the right time. You're not correcting the presenter. You're simply seen to be adding your weight to a key point.

Your prospect will appreciate the fact that you're helping each other and it's a pretty good real time example of how you work together as a team. The prospect will know how tough this is for you, so seeing you handle a problem will be a good test of the kind of people you are.

AWKWARD MOMENTS

Since you should have already anticipated many of the questions that the prospect might ask you, you should be well prepared for the interrogation. You also know who among your team is the right person to answer particular questions in their specialist area. You've established that you will field all questions and feed them out to the person most able to answer. However, there are almost always a couple of tough questions that you haven't anticipated. Your ability to handle these will play a part in how well your pitch comes off.

The first thing to emphasise here is, if you don't know the answer, say so. Tell them that you'll get back to them tomorrow. If it's a question that you should know the answer to, but don't, then don't try and fake an answer. You just have to say the truth, which is that 'I should know the answer to that, but I don't'. Human beings are like that—we can make mistakes. Prospects will let you make mistakes. But they will not let you tell a lie.

This is an issue of credibility. You can't be very credible or slightly credible. You are either credible or you're not. Credibility doesn't come from always telling the truth. Credibility comes from not lying. You can lose credibility very quickly if you try and fake an answer to a question, when you really don't have an answer. When we don't know an answer but try to battle through we fill the space where the right answer should go with words—lots and lots of words. The more we talk the worse it gets.

You can lose credibility in remarkably simple ways. If, as they are leaving, you are asked, 'Is it raining outside?', the correct answer isn't yes or no, unless you've looked out the window. The correct answer is 'It was/wasn't last time I looked'. There is a world of difference, and in that difference lies the fragile beating heart of your credibility.

BE FLEXIBLE

While you believe you have the right answer to solve their problem, they might not feel so good about it. However, they might love everything else about you except for your final answer. In which case, you need to find a way to be flexible about the solution you offer. The truth is it's just as easy to buy you and your business, without buying the answer you've provided.

Therefore, be careful about how dogmatic you are. You really don't know enough about their business. Pitches are unlike the real world. And as we have emphasised all the way through this book, the brief is not always the real problem.

What you are doing is giving them the best answer you possibly can to the question you've been given. But what the prospect is looking for is a business partner they can work with continuously, not just in answering one question. Therefore, don't paint yourself into a corner with your answer. You don't want to get to a point where they have to accept what your answer is or nothing.

In the advertising business we used to have a saying that went, 'You can't do great ads for clients you haven't got'. That is the dumb but simple truth. It's no good having a really great idea that solves their problem if the prospect doesn't want it. Better to get the business and work with them on the answer that you both can live with.

The same truth applies to any business that you pitch or tender for. It's very possible that the prospect can fall in love with you and your team, without loving the idea you've provided. So enter the presentation knowing that you have a great idea, but with enough flexibility to understand if the prospect doesn't like some part of the answer you can always change it later.

DIGGING OUT OF THE GRAVE

Once or twice in our experience there have been pitches that were doomed from the beginning. Maybe it was in the stars, but for whatever reason the pitch begins badly and just gets worse. There is really no disguising the fact that you and your team are dying and nothing is going to save you.

We once did a pitch where we were about to reveal the celebrity we thought would be the ideal vehicle to launch the prospect's brand, but one slide before the reveal the main client said, 'Just as long as it isn't that bastard (our celebrity) because I can't stand him'. Oh dear.

Another time a pitch went down in folklore for being the most inept ever made by our business. After the pitch, we looked at each other and just laughed. We knew that we'd all been hopeless. We rang the client on his car phone and said 'That was the worst presentation we have ever done!'. He agreed with us. So we said, 'So it's not a complete waste of time for you, give us twenty-four hours and we'll be back to you in your office with a half-hour presentation'. It saved the day for us and for the client, and now 'if it only saves you once a year, it's a good year'.

In the second example, the Pitch Leader stopped the presentation in its tracks. He said, 'Sorry, I'm going to stop right there. This simply isn't good enough. Can I ask that you give us one hour of your time tomorrow and we will have a much better answer and a much better presentation?'

The client reluctantly agreed, we worked overnight, came up with a brilliant answer, saved the day and won the business.

The lesson is that if you are aware of a disaster looming you must do something to save the day. If you know you are going to die anyway you have nothing to lose. At the point where you feel there is an opening, stop the pitch and apologise. You will get points for courage and maybe even a few bonus points for not wasting their time. Then you've got to decide whether it can be resurrected or not. Do you feel that the chemistry was there but that the answer was wrong? Or the presentation just didn't have any drama? Maybe it can be saved. Don't die wondering.

BE FLEXIBLE TAKE TWO

Once in a while something extraordinary happens during the presentation—the top judge clearly expresses what they see as the answer to the problem. That this happens at all is usually because no one on the judging panel has thought to discuss the issues of the brief with this key person until the actual day itself.

So the top judge gives you their spin on the solution. It's very likely that this may be a complete surprise to the other judges as well—otherwise you would have found this out in your discovery phase earlier in the process. The question is what do you do about it, given the great possibility that the answer the key judge has in his head may not be the answer you have loaded into your PowerPoint?

That all depends on how big the issue is. If they're simply stating an opinion, it is possible that you can easily argue them around to your way of thinking, using the evidence of your presentation to do it. You will naturally need to reflect their point of view as you pitch your answer, because to ignore their solution would be tantamount to ignoring them, and you can't do that. But just possibly you might be able to 'on the fly' add a little something to your solution that actually incorporates their idea.

ASK FOR THE ORDER

There is a remarkable fact about selling. It's based on the quote by ice hockey legend, Wayne Gretzky: 'You miss 100 per cent of the shots you never take'. Never ever fail to ask for the order. Take that shot.

In selling door to door the most successful salespeople know that they achieve 80 per cent of their sales not on the first or second call, not even on the third or fourth, but on and after the fifth call. They have to be dogged and undaunted. But they know that they have to keep taking the shot to succeed. In your case you only have one shot. Don't miss the chance to take it.

Selling is about asking for the business, yet people in business can be a little shy about being so nakedly commercial. But let's face it, that's what the prospect is there for, to give you their business. All you have to do is prove you deserve it, and once you've done that, ask nicely but forcefully for the order to proceed. Only once in one hundred times will you actually get the nod there and then, but you need to make them know how much you need to work with them. They need to be certain that you are hungry, so don't leave them in any doubt.

THE WONDERFUL TRUTH

What it all comes down to is this—in the end people buy people. If they like you, they will tend to like what you have to say and they will believe you can provide what they are looking for. Sure, you will need to be able to deliver on your promises and have the support to get the job done. And of course there will need to be a great answer to their brief (though it doesn't have to be the 'right' answer). But given all that, the wonderful truth is you only have to be yourself to be a success.

As long as you know everything there is to know about them, and how to work with them, the rest of it is easy. Just be yourselves, which means relax and enjoy the show.

Remember that although this is important, nobody dies. Keep it in perspective and just have fun. You'll like yourself a lot more, and chances are so will the prospects you're talking to.

{ epilogue }

it's not over until we say it's over

'We didn't lose, it just became a longer pitch.'
Ian Elliot

After the pitch, generally as soon as possible the following day, get in contact with whoever is appropriate from their team. From the pitch you would have worked out pretty clearly who the Key Decision Maker/s is/are. You would also have given yourselves the opportunity to get in contact with them via an answer to a question or two that needed elaboration. (Make sure you have at least one question that requires a deeper answer.) When you go back to them, you will also have the chance to correct any misconceptions that you felt may have crept into the pitch. These would be highlighted in your debrief from the Scribe.

Was there anything that didn't work? Is there a way to amplify the answer that now gives a stronger solution than you had yesterday—based on the information you received in the pitch itself? It may be something that one of the judges said that you can add in now as part of your solution that you didn't have yesterday. Whatever you can do to improve the solution based upon the information you now have—do it.

Now you have a complete picture of what are their hot buttons, what they loved, what they were cool about, what interested them and what they didn't like at all. You've discussed it with the Scribe who has downloaded all of the observations that they saw. What worked in their opinion? What was a touchy issue?

You now have far better knowledge than you ever had before. That's why we say that the pre-pitch and pitch is only about 70 per cent of the available points. Post-pitch is where you can really fine-tune your answer, getting closer and closer to what they really want.

Some people are squeamish about doing this kind of thing. They think they've done their job when the pitch ends. They also lose more often than they win. You have to take every advantage going.

Now you know pretty much all there is to know, short of working with them. Take every chance you can to give them the answer you now think they want. If it isn't the answer that you had yesterday, work out another one, that maybe evolves from that answer. They won't give you two bites at the cherry, obviously. But if you come back with a better, more refined thought, or a more specific solution to a now more clearly defined problem—well, isn't that what they really want?

TRIPPING UP THE COMPETITION

This is also the time to trip up the competition. Remember you don't just come first by being the best. You can also come first by ensuring that the guy who was neck and neck with you falls over before the finish line. This can be done through the intelligence you gathered at the pitch. Maybe they mentioned something they saw, or maybe you've heard something on the grapevine.

Don't be afraid to find a way to undermine the possible answer that the other guys may have given. Do it as subtly as you can of course. Innuendo is all that might be needed. Or a well-placed leak to the press.

Whatever it takes to win short of larceny is fine. After all, most of the time no one on the judging panel really has much of a clue what the really, really right answer is anyway. So all you are doing is helping them love your solution, and you can help that process along by getting them to fall out of love with your competitor's answer.

GETTING BAD NEWS AND USING IT

Sometimes you will lose—hard to believe but true. When you lose, what do you do? We have heard some people have actually sworn at the bearer of the bad news. This is not a good idea. The client may find that they can't proceed with their first choice for any number of reasons. And when they said (as they always do), 'It was very, very close, but you didn't win. But you were very near the mark', they might actually mean it this time. So you would be the next cab off the rank if you hadn't told them to take a running jump.

However, if you do come second and there is no denying it, be very thankful for their candour and ask them if it's at all possible to get some feedback on the presentation you gave. This is always flattering for the person doing the calling and in almost every case we've experienced they agree to tell you what went right and wrong and why.

This is good for two reasons. First, you get the best possible review of your methods and your people. Second—and here's the kicker—you get told exactly how to go about winning the pitch next time! They will always give you more than you ask for in the feedback and you will discover what it was that really worked for them. What did they love? What were their really key issues?

All this gives you a wonderful starting point for another discussion in about twelve months time, when the poor bastards who won the pitch have passed through their honeymoon period and the harsh dawn has lit upon their tired features and unhappy circumstances. Then you can come bounding in with a brilliant new solution for whatever it was they were after, with a much greater chance of success. Also, it keeps you in contact all that time as well. As Ian said, on those occasions (22.1 per cent of the time) when we didn't win: 'We didn't lose, it just became a longer pitch'.

AH, BUT IF YOU WIN!

Throw a party. When that wonderful magical call comes through, or more likely when the beaming prospect lights upon your doorstep with the good news, be very, very thankful. Make sure the messenger knows you are absolutely thrilled with this news. They may not want to stay for the champagne, but then again they might. And of course you do have champagne on hand for just such a moment.

Now you want to celebrate with all your staff. Winning is the lifeblood of business and the moment of winning is like your grand final. But unlike footy teams who only get lucky once a year at best, you can enjoy the euphoria as many times as you win. It's up to you to decide how often the champagne gets cracked.

{ positive thinking }

We firmly believe that you get what you foresee.
Visualise victory and you'll get it. Focus on
failure and you'll get it. Playing to win is a whole
different approach to playing not to lose.

Adversity and extremis brings out the best in
almost everyone. Winston Churchill said at the
height of the London Blitz, 'They do not know
it yet, but this will be the time of their lives'.
It brings people together for a common goal,
and can transform a company. But it takes
someone to have the courage to get up and say
it, and mean it.

{ the last word }

take it from a Harrow boy

The last word on this comes from Winston S. Churchill. Too many people have muddled up the truth of the story and claim that he got up at the Harrow School speech day and only said these nine wonderful words before sitting down again. He didn't, these nine words were part of a thirty-minute address. However, their power endures as representing one of the great mottos of all time and, as something that should be engraved over the door of every winning business, they are:

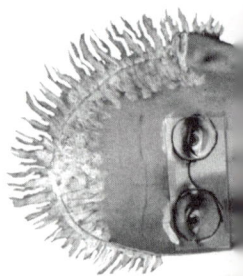

Never give in, never give in.
Never, never, never ...

Winston S. Churchill

{ appendixes }

appendix 1: meeting rules

'When the outcome of a meeting is to have another meeting, it has been a lousy meeting.'
Herbert Hoover

1.   A meeting needs to have a definite start and finish time; not starting fifteen minutes late or when everyone finally gets there. It can't be allowed to trickle on over the allotted span. Arriving late says you don't respect the people in the meeting or its purpose. Going over time means you're sloppy.

2.   Every meeting must have a leader. In pitches the leader of the meeting can either be the Pitch Leader or the Pitch Manager. But someone is in charge of the room and everything that happens in it.

3.   Every meeting has an agenda. Our friend John Vamos of Business Thinking Systems famously says, 'A meeting without an agenda achieves everything on it'. An agenda gives people comfort and it lays out who says what. It also shows that someone has actually thought about why you're having this meeting. Which leads us to ...

4.   It must have a purpose. And that purpose is clearly understood going into the meeting. That in turn means ...

5.   Everyone knows why they are there. There are no empty suits or wasted energy. If you are in the meeting there is a really good reason why you're there and not back at the coal face.

6. It has a conclusion. Which means that after the allotted time people know what has been accomplished. The leader of the meeting clarifies any issues and ensures that the purpose of the meeting was achieved. No one says, 'What was that all about?'

7. There are outcomes that people are responsible for. People leave the meeting with an ironclad understanding that anything that fell out of the meeting that must be followed up has been given to someone specifically. No one has any doubt about what they must do next.

Those are the absolute essentials for a quality meeting. If you don't follow them you just have discussions, not meetings.

A FEW MORE WORDS ON MEETINGS

Along with those cast iron rules there are a number of things that the meeting leader needs to be always aware of which are the *softer* meeting rules. Here they are.

Be Participatory

While there will always be a leader at each of these meetings, it's vital that everyone in these meetings understands that they are meant to participate. When everyone feels comfortable being able to express an opinion, you know you've got a far better chance of hearing every possible idea.

Be Enabling and Facilitating

The timeline meetings have got to have outcomes, therefore the participants have got to have the clear understanding that whatever is decided will be facilitated. They need to know the business will fast-track whatever needs to be done to enable the players to do or get whatever is required.

Be Smart with People's Time

Every meeting has to have the right people in it. How often have you thought to yourself, 'I don't need to be in this meeting'? A lot of times we bet. So it's vital that great care is given at the start of the process to put the right time in the right diaries. If a key player is asked to a meeting, they've got to know they have a vital role to play. Because you can bet that if you waste their time, then next time a timeline meeting is in their diary they won't be quite so interested in turning up.

Be Able to Mobilise Resources and Expertise

You're going to want certain things on certain days on the timeline. How often have you needed a PowerPoint presentation to be performed with precision only to find that either no one can find the right equipment, or no one has the expertise to run the damn thing? Your timeline pre-planning must guarantee that you get what you want when you want it. That means the right people with the right equipment, right on time.

Be Transparent

Every meeting needs to have a clear and understandable goal and a clear and easily communicable outcome. That means be transparent. Don't hold things back, give clarity to every participant. Which brings us to ...

Be Accountable

To us this simply means that if the outcome of the previous meeting was dependent upon you, you've done it—or else. Everyone needs to be held accountable, because everyone needs to see that they are working in a team environment that offers no excuses for failure. Accept no excuses for your team, or for yourself.

Don't Control—Do Regulate

As a leader of the business, or as the leader of the meeting, it's easy to become too dominant in a timeline meeting, especially if you have a clear end in mind. But you must steer clear of being too controlling. If you *control* people, you effectively stifle their creativity and their willingness to contribute. Whereas if you *regulate* them, you allow them to be creative, to shine, but they know there are clear guidelines to follow—for instance they only have five minutes to talk, or their expertise is required in this specific area.

Finally, Be Able To Take Ownership of Recommended Actions

This means the individuals who have been given the tasks to complete at the end of the meeting are responsible for the completion of those tasks. But they won't be able to take ownership if there are impediments in their way. So they have to be clearly given the authority to spend money or take whatever action is needed, without any fear that their actions will be later played back against them. If they are given ownership of the task, they must know that the full confidence and commitment of the company (and you) is behind them..

appendix 2: leadership

'Do what you can, with what you have, where you are.'
Theodore Roosevelt

There have been hundreds of books written about leadership. This isn't another one. This book is about winning. But winning in business requires someone to step up and be a leader. This could have been the first chapter in the book because having a great leader makes everything much easier. Now it's the last thing you might read, and perhaps it might inspire you to step up and be the leader you can be.

We've boiled it down to what we think are the relevant bits that can be applied to winning business. Because what we want to talk about is what leadership means in the context of the business of winning business. As with everything else in this book, the only purpose is to make it clear what is necessary to win. And having a leader who knows what it takes to be a leader is the most important thing of all.

General Norman Schwarzkopf defined leadership as the ability 'to inspire people to willingly do that which they ordinarily would not do'. In the annals of history there are hundreds of wonderful examples of leaders having that ability. There are great leaders of armies, great leaders of countries, great leaders of religious faiths, great leaders of businesses and great leaders of thought. So have you ever wondered what it takes to be a great leader? Are there characteristics that all the great leaders share, and if there are, how do you use them to your advantage—assuming that you too want to be a leader?

Well, there are distinct characteristics that leaders have that separate them from the ruck. They fall under four simple headings:
 - Their Character
 - Their Vision
 - Their Behaviour
 - Their Confidence

THEIR CHARACTER
The American Declaration of Independence states the mythic words: 'all men are created equal'. And the great leaders know it. This simply means that great leaders treat everyone they meet in the same way, as equals. It also has the built-in need for the true leader to see themselves as equal in all dealings with others, even if they may be far more significant figures in commerce or government. The great leaders have the ability to rise to the occasion and act accordingly.

Equally, the ability to see the same basic qualities in all people, whatever their station, is a key to a leader's humanity. Haven't you seen people treat their subordinates with little respect, while they act with sycophancy to those above them? That kind of person will never be a leader. Sure they might get the title, but they won't do the job. It comes down to a basic respect for the humanity in all of us, and great leaders have it.

So beware the person who 'kicks down and smiles up'.

Business is Fun

Compared to the really important things in life, business is just business. So it pays to keep things in perspective. In our business nobody dies. Have a sense of humour and use it.

Apart from the fact that everyone appreciates a leader who can laugh at themselves when necessary, it also gives permission for everyone else to have as much fun as possible. And in a world that can be pretty cheerless, having a laugh and having fun are a vital way to create a team harmony that you won't get if everyone feels like a grunt.

More than this, a leader who has the ability to see the lighter side of things makes it easier on everyone else. It lifts the spirits when you hear laughter coming from the corner office (if you happen to believe in corner offices, that is).

Leader Know Thyself

If you can't be honest with yourself, who can you be honest with? In fact we think that's why golf is such a great business tool, because it teaches a lot about not just your opponents but about you. There was a survey done recently which said that 80 per cent of business golfers think their opponents cheat, while 37 per cent said they have cheated themselves. That's remarkable. And shameful. Apart from the fact that golf is a very ethical game, it is just a game. And if the end result of cheating is winning, isn't that too high a price to pay?

So if you find yourself in the rough, and you give the ball a bit of a kick, you better know that you're a cheat and nothing else matters; no excuse is good enough. The same goes in terms of your other strengths and weaknesses. Whether they are character-based or skills-based.

Character-based weaknesses are the hardest to fix. If you know that you have a failing, it pays to understand how others see that failing. A lack of integrity is impossible to overcome. Your people will never trust you and no failing is greater.

Taking advantage of the perks of high office, while a little is fine, can lead people to cross the line. And you know when you cross it. We've all seen the damage that's been done to the role of the CEO by the various scandals in the United States and here in Australia. Ambition is good, greed isn't.

Then there is the urge some leaders have to keep the credit for themselves. It's easy when you've got the power to simply grab all the glory for yourself. Much better to deflect the praise to the people who deserve it. Especially if those people are further down the line.

Skills-based weaknesses are simpler to see and simpler to fix. The great leaders know where they have advantages and where they need help. They maximise those strengths and work on the weaknesses.

People give great respect to leaders who admit to a weakness. No one ever expects infallibility, and the fact that a leader will admit they need help in a certain area actually serves to underline their strengths for others. Because their team will be even more certain that the leader knows what they're doing in those areas under his command. But that doesn't mean you're allowed to keep that weakness, you've got to work on it if you expect others to work on theirs.

The Door is Always Ajar

'Management by walking around' may not be the best way to run a business, but it is the best way to create a personality that feels safe and approachable to the people who work for you.

In the past, too many leaders kept themselves locked behind big wooden doors, hidden from view and protected by frightening PAs. Those days are past. The leader needs to be seen. Plus it's vital that the leader has the ability to listen to the opinions of others, and that those opinions are valued.

If there is a climate of fear where subordinates don't feel comfortable broaching a subject, then pretty soon it will be difficult to find anyone who will tell you the truth. They'll just give you back what you want to hear. Honest feedback is needed on both sides of the management fence. Also, the attitude that suggests you are open to new ideas is invigorating for all who work with you. So keep that door ajar, don't leave it closed.

Keep Your Mind Ajar as Well

If you have a mind that's at least ajar to what your competitors are doing you should never be caught unawares. Lack of respect for an opponent has lost many a battle and many a winning pitch.

The ability to think like your competitors, to get inside their heads and see what they're seeing from their perspective, is one of the great talents of great leaders. Wellington described it as the ability 'to see what is on the other side of the hill'. Then, if you can translate that knowledge of the way your competitor is thinking, and learn from it, the better it is for you. Almost all of Sun Tzu's *The Art of War* is based on this point.

Don't Just Stand, Deliver

The very best leaders are very much 'can do people'. But they have a clear goal that they are aiming towards.

We don't much believe in mission statements, because they are usually mush created to make people feel better rather than give anyone a direction to head in. The best leaders give people a very clear purpose in mind and they are action-oriented, so that they take personal charge of heading towards that goal. Which brings us to our next point on leaders ...

THEIR VISION

In 1962, when President Kennedy responded to the Soviet lead in the space race, he didn't say, 'We're sending a rocket into space'. He said,

'We choose to go to the moon in this decade'. This is a compelling vision with a worthwhile end—and it's measurable. So everyone is very clear what they're all here for and what is to be achieved.

They also know that it's a win or a loss; there is no middle ground. And the leader has nailed their reputation to that objective. It's a lot easier to get people to walk behind you if they recognise the flag you're carrying and believe and *understand* the goal you're heading towards.

How many people have you worked for who have never clearly told you the actual objective they have in mind, in a way that is crystal clear in your mind? And when you worked for someone who had a clear vision, wasn't it easier to feel a part of the effort, and to make the sacrifices required? Well, that's the whole point of having a clear vision in the first place. That's why mission statements usually don't work, because they're too feelgood—where everything is covered off in adjectives and adverbs that render the central purpose obscure or generic. Create a vision for your winning business effort which is clear and unambiguous, because that's what the great leaders do. And have the courage to be measured by it.

Clarity of Command

One of the central themes that came through in our reading on great leaders is the clarity with which they've communicated their vision. Their orders are clear, there is little room for misunderstanding. Famously, Wellington's orders (written on the skin of an ass!) were always perfect examples of clarity of purpose and clear thinking.

He knew exactly what he was doing and he was able to clearly explain to his subordinates what was required. Ulysses S. Grant was equally succinct. Most great commanders have this same characteristic.

It works the same in business leadership. People need to be absolutely certain of the orders they need to carry out. No confusion, no uncertainty. Yet how often can you remember being in meetings or having discussions where at the end of it no clear plan was laid out and no outcome was agreed upon?

People find security in knowledge. If they have a specific action that they are responsible for, they should be held accountable for it. If they don't understand the order, they can be excused for failing. They must never be given that chance.

THEIR BEHAVIOUR

When the objectives outlined above have been clearly communicated by the leader, the outcomes will mainly depend on what the leader will do, and how they will behave.

Lend Me Your Army

In the American Civil War, the leader of the Union Armies, General George McClennan, was a notorious vacillator. He overestimated the strength of his enemies to such a degree that his army was rendered inactive. He had a plan, and a clever one, but he never had the capacity, personally, to put that plan in to action—he wasn't action-oriented. So much did this pain President Lincoln that he sent off a gentle but potent telegraph that simply asked, 'If you don't want to use the army I should like to borrow it for a while'.

The great leaders find it difficult to rationalise inaction. They want to get things done. And having achieved action, they are relentless in their follow-up. They are on the tail of the enemy. They are also in constant contact with their people to ensure that every opportunity is being taken to press home the advantage. And again, none of this is possible unless there is a clear goal in mind. 'How's it going?' is a pretty lame question if no one knows where they're going.

Take Charge and Take Change

Change is a fearful thing, it means that something has to happen. That's why it's important to understand the effect that any change you suggest in your winning presentation is fully considered for all parties involved in the decision-making process. People are frightened by change. They'd rather do nothing. They feel safer right here where they are.

But of course we know change is inevitable and great leaders embrace it—they don't believe the argument that starts, 'But we've never done that before ...' In fact, one of the great examples of leadership embracing change is the Nokia phone company. Originally a maker of paper products, they expanded into making galoshes, tyres and raincoats.

In the middle 1980s the Finnish Government was at the forefront of in-car telephony, and Nokia decided to move into electronics. During the deep depression of the early 90s they even briefly considered selling to Ericsson; instead they decided to enter the mobile hand-held market. Their first product was intended to sell 400,000 units—it sold 20 million, and in the process changed the world. They didn't fight change, they embraced it.

On the other hand, in 1983 AT&T asked McKinseys to give them a point of view on the whole idea of portable telephones. McKinseys (and we're not poking the finger at them, these things happen) said that in their opinion, by the year 2000, there would be a worldwide market for approximately 900,000 portable (mobile) phones. In other words, don't change, do nothing.

AT&T did nothing, until 1993, when they got back into the mobile business when they bought the McCaw mobile communications business for US$5.3 billion. Great leaders help create and shape change. They have no fear. And they take their team with them on the journey.

Do Today and Think of Tomorrow

Understanding that change is inevitable and positive means that the attitude of the great leader is one that seizes opportunities that are available right now, yet doesn't compromise on the need to invest in the future.

The investment can be in people or technology, or in planning or any number of other ways to stay ahead of the game. The only vital thing is that the great leader knows that the future is theirs to build, rather than to react to. And they have the courage to do it.

There are no Boundaries

The key thing for the great leader is simply this: they are judged by their results. They tend to flourish in an environment that has no boundaries, either physically or mentally. They have the ability to see the big picture and don't think or act in any kind of mental box. Because results are everything (and let's face it, these days there is nothing else), then if you're a smart leader you really don't care who gets the credit for the results you're after, as long as they are achieved.

Anything is possible if you have an attitude that is open-hearted and open-handed. One of the wonderful concepts in Stephen R. Covey's book *The 7 Habits of Highly Effective People* is the idea that if you have a feeling of abundance, and you share that feeling, you tend to get abundance in return; while if your attitude is that there is little enough to share, and you want to keep it all for yourself, you will tend to get less and less. We really believe in being open-hearted and seeing the world in a positive light, which leads to ...

Think Positive

One of the great quotes by Winston Churchill that underlines the power of positive thinking was written on the night he became Prime Minister of Great Britain. While no one could have foreseen the dangers in the days and weeks ahead, anyone would have had grounds for pessimism. The British expeditionary forces were in extremis in France, the German army's juggernaut showed no signs of slowing, the French were on the verge of collapse, and the United States was in no hurry to come to the aid of Britain in this 'foreign war'.

In this climate, Churchill wrote: 'as I went to bed at about 3 am I was conscious of a profound sense of relief ... although impatient for the morning. I slept soundly and had no need for cheering dreams. Facts are better than dreams'. How wonderful to be so full of confidence, so secure in the certain knowledge that now events were under his control.

It is also interesting that the other candidate for the job, Halifax, the 'Holy Fox', rejected it before it was offered to Churchill. Even the King had no great faith in this failed and old (65 at the time) politician. Yet now we know that Churchill and his leadership changed the course of the war.

So perhaps that may be a supreme example of thinking positive, but of course there are so many others, inspiring in their own way. From the heroism of men like Christopher Reeve and wheelchair triathlete John Maclean, to the profound story of Helen Keller or the struggle and triumph of Nelson Mandela. Yet the same galvanising effect can be achieved in business, if the leader shows that basic optimism.

We've been fortunate to work with a number of great leaders, and one of the key factors in their success has been a simple tenacity—the ability to never give up. It's a character trait that motivates their behaviour in every area of their life. They will not be beaten.

'You mean there's a chance?!' Unlimited optimism is a wonderful thing. A great and funny example of it can be found in the movie *Dumb and Dumber*, starring Jim Carrey. There's a scene where we see Jim Carrey's character rehearsing his lines for how he will declare his undying love to the beautiful and unattainable woman of his dreams. She interrupts him and he tries to deliver the lines, but it all comes out wrong, and the scene is quite pathetic as this dweeb declares his passion for this vision of beauty.

Finally after struggling and failing he simply says, 'What's the chance of you and me being together?' She's as gentle as she can be and demurs. He tries again, 'Is it one in a hundred?' She has to answer honestly, 'Well no'. He keeps trying, 'One in a thousand?' Again, no. Finally, she answers, 'More like one in a million'. At this Carrey pauses, takes it in and a smile begins to stretch across his face as he gleefully declares, 'So you're telling me there is a chance!!!!'. If you can capture that kind of optimism, you have a better than one in a million chance of being a great leader, because you will never ever give up.

The Trees and the Forest

Great leaders take pains. It's said that the Battle of Waterloo was lost by Napoleon because he suffered from piles and failed to reconnoitre the ground on the night before the battle. The truth is probably not so prosaic. He relied on his generals and General Ney on that occasion failed him. Ney and the weather. It almost always rained on Wellington's battles.

Wellington did prepare for the Battle of Waterloo, however, and in fact chose the field of battle in August of 1814, fully ten months before 18 June 1815. Now that's a man who is detail-oriented.

But while the great leaders are detail-focused—just enough to know that each of the objectives are being met—they also have an understanding of the bigger picture, never delving too deeply into the minutiae at the expense of the end result they have in mind.

'We Have Nothing to Fear but Fear Itself'

Fear is self-defeating. In the leader fear manifests itself most obviously in a fear of making decisions, because their decisions can prove costly—in war, with the loss of blood, the loss of battle and the loss of the war itself. In business, it's fear of failure. The fear that, 'If I do this, then that may happen, so maybe it's better to do nothing'.

It also manifests itself in a need to get consensus for all decisions. If you fear going out on a limb, then you won't be a great leader. Somebody has to make the big decisions and that's the leader.

Certainly, listen to all points of view, certainly discuss issues where you feel you lack expertise or experience, but in the end, don't be afraid to fail. It's best summed up in the pithy 'Discuss often, decide once'. And once you've made up your mind follow the maxim of Rupert Murdoch, whose personal motto is 'No Regrets'. He seems to have done fine, so perhaps you could adopt that same attitude.

Just as importantly, you must allow your team to fail and allow them to learn from the failure. If your attitude gives people the freedom to try and fail, they will more than likely try harder, play smarter and win next time. Birds don't learn to fly first, first they learn to fall.

Keep Talking

People respond best when they get constant feedback. Working in a vacuum is a horrible place to be. Keep talking to everyone involved in the process as you head to your objective. That's what the great leaders do. You don't have to do it on the field of battle any more, but words of encouragement and appreciation are just as valued in business. Especially give constant reinforcement of the objective that needs to be achieved. The great leaders keep their teams clearly focused on that part of the plan that they can help achieve.

But don't simply speak; listen intently as well. You want to hear everything that's happening; you need to have a fully rounded picture and the only way that can happen is if you listen to your people. They will be able to give a 360-degree snapshot of the whole problem, and you in turn can give them feedback about what's working and what's not. And about ways of doing things differently to achieve your joint objective.

Remember that the team members who are most informed (within reason—they probably don't want to know your worries), are also likely to be the highest achievers—and will be the most motivated to deliver the outcome you want.

Set the Standard

In business as in war, the leader who walks the walk is the one most likely to be respected. That means the effort must be visible, and your team needs to see that you are just as exacting on yourself as you are on them. You are willing to put yourself in harm's way for the good of the team. Get involved, get your hands dirty, make changes and make decisions. In other words, lead.

Act with Confidence and Trust

The final part of the leadership equation is to act with confidence and trust. And like almost everything in the leadership spectrum, it feeds on itself for good or ill. If you have confidence in yourself and your team, and you show it, then the trust will follow.

Equally, if you are reticent or lack the courage to make decisions, the trust will fade away and die.

We tend to believe that confidence and trust lead to success which in turn builds confidence and trust and goes on and on in a never-ending cycle. If you are willing to walk 'shoulder to shoulder, no light between', your team will follow you anywhere you choose to lead them.

But also, it's about the ability to compel rather than command and the ability to influence rather than control. To compel someone to do something means you are a force driving them irresistibly to their goal, but they still have the task in their control. To command means you are ordering someone to do something; it's out of their control. Similarly, to influence someone into an action is quite different and more empowering for them than to exert control over them.

These are subtle but important differences that determine the success or failure of leadership.

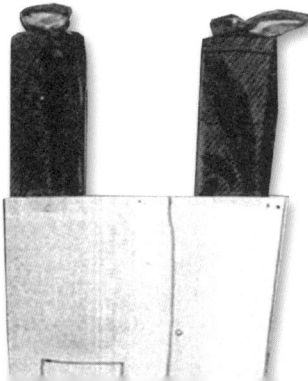

First published in 2007 by Pier 9, an imprint of Murdoch Books Pty Limited

Murdoch Books Australia
Pier 8/9
23 Hickson Road
Millers Point NSW 2000
Phone: +61 (0)2 8220 2000
Fax: +61 (0)2 8220 2558
www.murdochbooks.com.au

Murdoch Books UK Limited
Erico House
6th Floor
93–99 Upper Richmond Road
Putney, London SW15 2TG
Phone: +44 (0) 20 8785 5995
Fax: +44 (0) 20 8785 5985

Chief Executive: Juliet Rogers
Publishing Director: Kay Scarlett

Concept and Design: Reuben Crossman
Project Manager and Editor: Emma Hutchinson
Production: Maiya Levitch

National Library of Australia Cataloguing-in-Publication Data
Kellard, Marty.
Stop bitching start pitching : the 9 success steps to winning business.

ISBN 978 1 921208 88 1.
ISBN 1 921208 88 0.

1. Business enterprises - Marketing. 2. Success in
business. 3. Business planning. I. Elliot, Ian, 1953- .
II. Title.

650.1

Printed by Midas Printing (Asia) Limited in 2007. PRINTED IN CHINA.
Reprinted 2007.

we wish you the best
of luck ...

but now, you won't need it.